The
Hypocrite
Within

Mayuran
Senthilnathan

Illustrations by Mahita Dasi

TATTVA
PRESS

First published in Great Britain in 2020 by Tattva Press

publishing@tattva.org.uk

www.tattva.org.uk

ISBN: 978-1998624-4-2

British Library Cataloguing in Publication Data. A catalogue record for this book is available from the British Library.

Printed and bound by Clays Ltd.

Dedicated to my
Spiritual Master
Paramahamsa Vishwananda

Contents

Preface – An Invitation to Look in the Cupboard

I remember when my spiritual Master, Paramahamsa Vishwananda, paid a surprise visit to my house some years ago. I had about ten minutes to transform my home from a bombsite into something vaguely respectable. In a blind panic I gathered all my clothes and rubble scattered around and threw them into a random cupboard. Eventually, my Master arrived and after some time He asked for a tour of the house. I began presenting all the different rooms which were now immaculately arranged. I was secretly quite proud of the fact that everything appeared in good order. Although it was a trivial matter, I was keen to gain His approval. As we were going round, He stopped in front of a cupboard – the same cupboard which had everything dumped inside it. When He asked me to open it, I subtly tried to distract Him with polite conversation, but He kept staring at it. Of all the cupboards in the house why did He have to pick this one? Despite my efforts to move Him on, He insisted again. There was no choice, so I opened the door and braced myself. Both my Master and I stood there looking at the horror of what was inside. Endless laundry, rubbish and toiletries were all there chaotically piled in a heap. I had spent the last hour parading how great and clean my home was and in an instant the truth of how I really lived had been exposed.

The incident was a small embarrassment with a profound lesson: If I want to know who I truly am, if I want to discover my purpose, I cannot bury things away and expect to genuinely progress. I must openly and directly engage with everything that is holding me back. I have to be willing to open the cupboard, deal with what is inside and rise above it. This book is an invitation to do exactly that. As we shall see, spiritual hypocrisy is fundamentally about the ego and how it manipulates us. This is why we need to recognise and understand it as clearly as possible – through awareness of the ego we can disarm it.

Whilst there are innumerable spiritual books discussing a variety of inspiring topics, it is rare to find one entirely dedicated to wrestling with the negativity we have within. My intention in writing this book is to alert seeking individuals to the many pitfalls we can all fall into on the spiritual path. Hypocrisy is not a subject we can deal with lightly; it must be tackled explicitly and precisely. It is for this reason I have not approached this in a half-hearted way but have instead done my best to dive right into the thick of the issues. I fully appreciate that it is not easy to read about one's own flaws. Acknowledging how we have been straying from where we ought to be, is difficult. At the same time, it is perhaps the most important practice we can do. This is what liberates us from negativity and returns us to a place of authenticity. It is what clears our path and frees us to be who we truly are.

In an effort to bring the different aspects of hypocrisy to life, I have used various personalities of the Mahabharata. For those who are unfamiliar with the narrative, the key events of the story most relevant to the discussion have been outlined. The Mahabharata is both an embellished historical account of events and also a wonderful work of spiritual literature. Added to this, it is a portal into the inner world, an illustration of what goes on within us.

It is worth noting that the complexity of the Mahabharata allows it to be looked at from many different levels and my interpretation is obviously not the only way of viewing it. Depending on the perspective we take and the situation we focus on, the characters can mean very different things. Most people tend to view this great epic through the deeds of the Pandavas. Their various trials and successes, as well as their relationship with Krishna are what people tend to dwell on. This book is different, in that it focuses on the characters who align with Duryodhana. He stands for the purest form of the ego. Those who have sided with him represent various archetypes of negativity that need to be defeated.

The different descriptions of the characters are deliberately strong and are an attempt to amplify the workings of the ego. So much of what it does is subconscious and unknown. Therefore, I have purposefully blown up the issues so that we can understand the subtleties that might otherwise be missed.

Each chapter begins with highlighting the desires and regrets of the personalities from the Mahabharata. Then there is a detailed description that relates the character to our inner world. We see how their qualities represent our psychology and how this dictates our behaviour. This is a crucial section where all the different traits of that particular form of the ego are laid out.

The descriptions are detailed, and at times intense. I would urge the reader to take their time and really reflect on the points made. The aim of these explanations is to put together a diagnosis of what may be going on inside us. Robustly revealing the nature of the ego is in itself a major part of the solution to hypocrisy. Just by recognising how it works we are given a chance to pause and restrain ourselves from being manipulated by the negative impressions we might carry.

Once we have understood what might be happening, at the end of every chapter, I have put forward some key Life Lessons to contemplate on. These are designed to give practical steps to help us escape the ego's influence. They summarise the key points and provide guidance on how we can start to deal with some of the issues raised. I would like to point out that each of these lessons is specific to the particular form of ego described and does not necessarily apply across other chapters. Because every manifestation of the ego is unique, it requires a specific way of dealing with it. As we shall see, what works for one aspect may not work for another.

While the Life Lessons in particular, can help us move forward, it is in the final chapter where we find the ultimate solution to spiritual hypocrisy. As one moves through the different personalities of the Mahabharata, it gradually becomes clear that the ego has so many disguises. Everywhere we turn, there is the potential for it to control us. The immediate and perhaps natural response for some is to feel dejected and hopeless. What chance do we have of evolving if everything we think and do can be unconsciously used by the ego? Believe it or not, this state is actually quite healthy and can be used to our advantage. The last character of Draupadi shows how the state of helplessness can transform us. It allows us to see the world and ourselves in a completely different way. This is what opens us up to the grace of the Divine.

Writing a book about hypocrisy does not mean I, myself, am somehow aloof from the subject matter. Anyone who has a mind bound to this world is going to be a hypocrite at some level. What has given me the confidence to write such a book is the experiences I have had with my spiritual Master.

After some fifteen years of knowing Him, I have seen the transformative effect of real Divinity. I have learned that pure Love does not pander to the ego, it compels us to rise above it. The Master presents to us the limitations we have. He awakens the longing to grow, He supports and inspires us to develop. Ultimately, we have the choice to resist change or embrace it. I have repeatedly witnessed the workings of the ego in myself and in other individuals around the Master. While everyone's personal situations may vary, it almost always involves the same old patterns coming up. Through the lens of the Mahabharata I have compiled these patterns together so we can all understand and learn how to spot them.

My Master has shown me that we all have a Divine purpose, and it can be attained. This, in itself, is a life changing revelation. In addition, He has also revealed the work that needs to be done to reach this goal. He has not taught me through mere words, but by direct experience. Through numerous encounters with Him, I have come to understand that there is no difference between the Master and life. It is the same Personality in a different form working to take us higher. The Master rests in our hearts, He is the Truth that never changes and the Love which never gives up on us.

The Ego – The Foundation of All Hypocrisy

How Important Is It to Be Truthful?

Each of us wears a mask. In fact, we wear several masks. Depending on the situation and the people around us, we choose which one to adorn. This is not as deceitful as it sounds; there is a social standard we have to be sensitive to. We cannot unleash every aspect of ourselves to every individual. Masks are needed for relationships to work; they are needed to guard parts within us that are precious and personal. The real question to ask is how many masks are we unconsciously wearing? In other words, how many are we wearing to shield ourselves from ourselves? What ideas are we clinging onto to cover up the reality of who we are? Why are we doing it and for what end?

The world we live in rarely demands answers to these questions. Whether it is performing in a job interview or being liked amongst friends, if we are charismatic enough, we can often get what we want without having to display who we truly are. Winning the opinion of others does not always demand honesty. Nobody is monitoring our inner world; our thoughts and intentions are hidden. We can relax and be our own moral policeman. Outwardly we have to deliver a personality that is pleasing, but within the confines of our mind and heart, we have the freedom to jump, dance and roam free.

If we are on the spiritual path, things could not be more different. Truth in its absolute purity is what we are striving for. Being on a spiritual path means our life is centred around self-development. Rather than pursuing what is easy and pleasurable, we are trying to discover the deepest and most fundamental part of who we are and make that our home. Walking a path means we have a clear goal, to discover the Truth. There is a strong desire to find a higher meaning. We have a yearning to answer the age old questions of Who am I? Why have I incarnated? and what is my purpose? The desire to realise what lies behind these deep enquiries is what makes us take up various practices, it is what makes us interested in different philosophies and it is what causes us to join various spiritual traditions. Within us, there is a conviction that beyond this world there exists something transcendent and Divine. The spiritual path is the journey to knowing that place first hand, it is where we commit to making this the focus of our life. Regardless of our specific beliefs, what remains consistent to any seeker of Truth is the need to be utterly honest with ourselves.

Our inner world which is concealed to others, is the very ground we are looking to walk. The aim of a spiritual seeker is to pierce the bubble of thoughts and emotions and find that state which is changeless and pure. Being sincere is not just useful on our path, it is the most essential quality to take us forward. Without it, the journey is over before it has even begun.

In many ways, how valuable something is can be measured by how sincere we have to be to attain it. Shallow friendships do not require integrity. We can fake who we are, we can laugh at jokes that are not funny, we can talk about issues that do not interest us, we can pretend we really care when we do not. As long as the other person is convinced, the game can go on. In contrast, sustaining meaningful relationships, requires authenticity. They do not withstand pseudo versions of who we are. The spiritual seeker is after the ultimate relationship – one with the Divine, and by definition this requires the ultimate level of sincerity. There is no room for any masks.

To experience this relationship, self-analysis is essential. We have to cut right through our psychological layers. It involves launching a campaign against preconceived ideas, challenging everything and taking nothing for granted. This can bring an immense amount of destruction. It can cause whole perspectives to break down and it can tear through facets of our personality we hold dear. We may define ourselves by our career, or by our talents, but these are just stories of who we think we are. Self-analysis aims to see through such stories to get to what is real. It is an attempt to pull back from false concepts and reclaim who we truly are – the soul, that which is divine and eternal. The more sincere we are, the closer we can get to it.

The amount of effort we invest in this process depends on how much we value what is true. How important is it to understand ourselves as we really are, versus how we think we are, or hope we might be? For some, it is utterly irrelevant. Life is to be enjoyed, and truth is just an inconvenient obstacle. For others, it might be good to have a deeper understanding of ourselves, but it is not critical to strive for. For those on a spiritual path, however, what is true cannot be a secondary goal, it has to be the fundamental basis upon which everything else flows. Without it, we cannot be sincere and we cannot love. To the seeker who wishes to know themselves, there is nothing more important.

Understanding the Personality, the Ego and the False Identity

Hypocrisy works on many levels. At the most superficial, there is a discrepancy between action and words - we fail to practice what we preach. From a spiritual perspective, hypocrisy is a much deeper affair; it is all about the various strategies of the ego. It is when we believe we are living up to one persona, but inwardly we have chosen another. It is when we have claimed to put Truth at the top of our hierarchy when, in fact, we have inadvertently placed the ego there. Using different narratives we subconsciously try to cover up the gap between who we think we are and who we really are. This often works at an incredibly subtle level which is difficult to detect. Before we can understand how this works, we need to know exactly what the ego is, where it comes from and how it is formed.

The Soul

At the very root of each of us, there is the soul. It is the changeless background behind all experience. It is existence itself. Although it empowers our mind and body, it has nothing to do with this material world. The soul is pristine and pure, as we grow in sincerity, we draw closer to it.

The False Identity

Covering the soul, is the false identity - the feeling of being an independent individual who belongs to this world. The false identity makes us wrongly assume that we are not Divine, that we are material beings who exist for a material purpose. It is incredibly subtle, but at the same time it is the foundation upon which we live all of life. Everyone has the sense of 'I', the belief that we are the doer, enjoyer and sufferer of what happens around us. Despite being fundamental to how we think and live, it is a lie. Like a lost lion living amongst a herd of sheep, we have become conditioned by this deep conviction and robbed of the Truth, that we are in fact an eternal part of the Cosmic whole. The false identity is the primal instinct that pushes us into activity and drama. It makes us calculate where we stand in relation to others and what we can and cannot claim as ours. It is the thing that makes us take our place in the world. The false identity is in short, the very bedrock upon which our whole personality is built.

From the moment we can perceive the world, various life experiences start to leave impressions in our psyche. The feeling of not being loved by our parents, the privileged upbringing that gave everything we wanted, the popularity and attention we received growing up or the lack of acceptance from so-called friends, are all examples of how such impressions are left in our subconscious. Over time, they gather together, and eventually a whole network of underground belief systems are created. Statements such as 'I am not good enough', 'I am talented', 'Nobody likes me' or 'I deserve better' start to rise up. Whenever we agree with them, even slightly, we end up reinforcing them.

These beliefs build up insecurities, fears, aspirations and fantasies which end up dictating our behaviour. Just as a cloud forms from the gathering of water vapour, this complex web of impressions creates an altogether separate entity known as the ego. The false identity provides the initial belief that we belong to the world, but it is the ego which emerges out of it and creates our self-image. It is, if you like, the active component of the false identity. It is where the sense of 'I' develops and dynamically responds to the experiences we have. The ego is constantly changing depending on what we face. The more we act out its impulses, the more cemented it becomes. When it is strong, it almost behaves like a separate entity. It has its own desires and plans that it wants to implement.

As we repeatedly give in the ego, it can end up completely controlling our behaviour. Somehow, it makes us try and get away with things we should not, it causes us to manipulate people around us, or feel resentment when we do not get our way. Over time these behavioural patterns become embedded and manifested in our personality.

Personality

The personality is what we show to others and what we superficially take ourselves to be. It is how we are perceived from a casual analysis. For instance, most of us are aware of how confident we are - we know whether we are outgoing or introverted. We are aware of what things excite or annoy us, and we may even have an idea about some of our insecurities. The more we analyse our personality, the deeper we can move into our psyche and see how the ego works. The less conscious we are, the more our personality acts out the ego's will with almost no awareness.

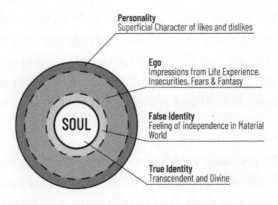

Personality
Superficial Character of likes and dislikes

Ego
Impressions from Life Experience, Insecurities, Fears & Fantasy

False Identity
Feeling of independence in Material World

True Identity
Transcendent and Divine

SOUL

As this happens, we can end up drifting into a kind of coma. Our behaviour and decisions become reflex based. Like a broken record, the same old subconscious belief systems dictate everything we are doing. We are not acting but reacting. The various impressions that make up the ego drag us into emotion and stop us honestly assessing what we are doing. Gradually we can end up becoming entirely subordinate to its demands.

The ego is like a virus - it evolves to survive. As soon as we think we have it worked out, it pops up in another disguise. One minute we may see it as a boastful arrogance that wants to be the centre of attention, the next it can swing to the other extreme making us retreat into fear and anxiety. We may try to bow our heads and be as humble as we can, but in attempting to do so we may end up becoming incredibly self-absorbed. Because the ego is so elusive, we may mistakenly think we have put Truth on the altar, but in reality, the Truth we worship is our ego in disguise.

The journey out of this game is the journey back to the soul. If our awareness is stuck at the level of personality, then almost all our inner conflicts will be unknown to us. The purpose of self-analysis is to know the realm of the ego and understand how it is working within us. This is what makes us more spiritually conscious. Instead of being a victim of all the impressions we have inside, we will be able to face and overcome them. As we move closer to the soul, we will be more authentic, we will reach the peak of sincerity and eventually realise our divine nature.

What Does the Ego Want?

Fundamentally the ego wants to survive. The false identity makes us believe we belong to this material world and it is the ego's duty to keep that belief alive. While our soul is driving us towards spiritual growth, the ego is desperate to keep us bound to the world. It pushes our vision outwards and reduces our ability to find inner wisdom. All of life becomes narrowly reduced to what we want and how we feel in the moment.

As well as wanting to survive, the ego wants to enjoy. Through a variety of methods it uses our personality to seek pleasure. Sometimes it is done through fame and glory. Other times it uses emotions such as self-pity or even a feeling of being righteous and good. The desire to survive and enjoy is often camouflaged through certain narratives. Statements such as 'I have no choice' or 'Everyone is against me' or 'This is what my duty is' all become useful to validate the ego's position.

When the Ego is Awoken

Unless we are particularly sharp, much of the ego will lie hidden. Only when circumstances disturb us does its presence start to surface. When the relationship we pinned everything on breaks down, when the life plan we wanted so badly starts to crumble, when we are denied attention and success, then we start to see how the ego operates. Like old mines that suddenly go off, our insecurities can blow up, exposing its presence.

This becomes clear when we see the irrationality in our behaviour. Things like being overly attached to people or being disproportionately hurt by innocent comments; are examples of the ego asserting itself. Its responses are complicated and hopelessly illogical. It makes our behaviour inconsistent and contradictory to the principles we say we hold. Somehow, despite our better judgement we can often end up defending the ego's cause. When something goes wrong, we shift the blame onto other people, or we tell ourselves that we have a right to feel the way we do. Different stories are used to protect our emotions and suppress truths we do not want to face. Whether through joy or sorrow, greed or sacrifice, the ego is trying one way or another to stop us marching forward.

Each of us is unbelievably complicated, and it takes effort to discover why we do what we do and why we think what we think. But if we can do it, we will be liberated from the burden of past impressions, fears and insecurities. We will heal old wounds that have been controlling our life.

The Need for Sincerity

Beyond the ego and even beyond the false identity, our soul is whispering for us to find the Truth - the deeper meaning to life. We may not know exactly what that is, but we know it is beyond this world. The whisper from within is what compels us to take up the spiritual path and make inner growth a priority. Despite what we are being told by society, friends and family, there is something urging us to gamble and see where this calling will take us. The ego does not want us to answer this call. Walking the spiritual path and finding the Divine are a direct threat to it, a danger that it wants to avoid at all costs.

But how exactly do we stop the ego from taking over? Is there some quick-fix technique that will give us immunity from this imminent danger? The answer is an emphatic 'no'. The irony is that sincerity is needed to protect sincerity. There has to be some kind of desire to be true to ourselves, some willingness to peer into the mirror and see what is nesting within. So long as we can muster the courage to do that, then there is always a way out of hypocrisy.

What is encouraging is that sincerity is a positive spiral. The more honest we can be with ourselves, the closer we will venture to the light of the soul and the more insight we will have going forward. The initial stages are difficult, but as momentum builds, clarity appears. Everybody has a seed of sincerity to follow their path, and like with any seed, when it is nurtured it becomes stronger. The ego, on the other hand, is like a weed. If left untreated it grows, and eventually spreads to every part of us.

When we can clearly see how our actions and thoughts no longer match our believed intentions, then the floodlights come on and our deception is exposed. Just like realising we are dreaming wakes us up, the revelation of insincerity shocks us out of our ego-centred illusion. When we have seen enough of our hypocrisy, naturally we will be compelled to change.

The Mahabharata – An Illustration of How the Ego Works

Within the vast corpus of Indian literature there are countless philosophical texts, devotional stories and historical accounts. The Mahabharata, however, stands out for its sheer beauty and breadth of knowledge. Spanning some 100,000 verses this immense work manages to discuss innumerable aspects of life. The nature of reality, devotion to God, yoga, the functioning of society, warfare and even diet are all touched upon. The Mahabharata itself makes the declaration that 'Whatever can be found here, may be found elsewhere, but whatever cannot be found here can never be found elsewhere.'[1] Amongst all this teaching, running at the heart of this scripture is the question 'What is dharma?'. We have all been given life for a reason, there is a purpose to our existence. What then is the proper way to live? dharma is based on the understanding that each of us has a certain role that we have to strive for and there is a cosmic order to align with. Dharma is not merely a moral code, it is the path we have been born to tread.

The Mahabharata explores the complexity of dharma by narrating the feud that rages within the Kuru royal family. The evil Kauravas headed by Duryodhana are bent on persecuting and robbing their cousins, the Pandavas, of their kingdom. The dispute climaxes in a great war where all the kings in the land choose their sides. What is particularly interesting are the characters who choose to side with Duryodhana. Each of them have their own vision of dharma and they use it to justify their stance. Despite knowing Duryodhana to be utterly selfish and cruel, they find a justification to serve him. Somehow, they conclude that righteousness involves championing his cause. Without any doubt, they believe wholeheartedly that they are on the right path.

It is through an analysis of these situations that we can gain real insight into the nature of spiritual hypocrisy. Just as Duryodhana manages to use these personalities to fight the Pandavas, the ego uses a variety of narratives to

[1] Mahabharata XVIII 5.50

control us. The different characters represent archetypal patterns that the ego adopts for survival and pleasure. The thoughts, emotions, and the various intentions of these personalities embody various traits we have within.

As we progress through the characters, we may sense a familiarity with them. This is because at some level we know them, we are aware of what our ego is doing, but through denial or fear, we have yet to bring that truth to the surface. Understanding this will shed new light on the Mahabharata. Not only will it remain one of the greatest stories ever told, it will be a gateway through which we can understand ourselves.

The Mahabharata – A Playing Out of Our Inner World

The great seer Vyasa sat in contemplation. After performing intense penance, he had analysed the immense body of Vedic knowledge. Endless amounts of spiritual writings had been organised and divided up, but yet he wanted to do more. In the ages to come, humanity needed something more accessible than philosophical truths. They needed to know how to live and to understand the complexities of the human condition. What is righteousness and what is virtue? What is love and what is selfish attachment? These are the questions that were most pressing. Vyasa sat back and thought about the various events that led to the great war between his grandsons, the Kauravas and the Pandavas. In his wisdom he peered into the psyche of each person without any judgement. He saw their desires, their emotions and their conflicting intentions. He remembered the various situations that pushed and pulled them to take decisions. He took no

sides, there was no bias, and in that perfect state of neutrality,
he poured forth the greatest of all poems.

Bhishma's Vow

Devavrata, the son of Ganga, was an exemplary prince
of Hastinapura. He was learned beyond compare and an
unbelievable warrior. A dramatic turning point came when
he saw his father, Shantanu, alone and grief-stricken. The
king had lost his heart to Satyavati, a fisherman's daughter
and was desperate to marry her and make her his queen. But
Satyavati's father was adamant that he would only agree,
if it were guaranteed that his daughter's children would be
next in line to the throne. Shantanu was distraught, for
there was no way he could deny his own son the kingdom
for the sake of this marriage. He simply had to suffer the
pain of separation for the rest of his life. Devavrata looked
upon his father and his miserable state pained him. He was
not content to let this situation stand. Without Shantanu
knowing, he journeyed to the fisherman's village and there
he took the most extreme of vows. He renounced his
claim to the throne and to ensure that none of his future
children would seize it in the future, he took an oath to
remain celibate and never marry. Whilst always protecting
the kingdom of Hastinapura, he would forsake power and
love. The celestial beings rained flowers upon him for this
tremendous sacrifice.

For a royal warrior, this was an unbelievable
commitment. From that moment he became known as

Bhishma – the one who had taken a terrible vow. Shantanu was overwhelmed with his son's devotion to him. With the strength of this immense gratitude, he gave a blessing that no matter what, Bhishma would be free to choose the timing of his death.

Dhritarashtra and Pandu Are Born

Years passed and eventually Shantanu passed away. The eldest son of Satyavati was crowned king but was tragically slaughtered in a duel. Although still very young, his brother took the throne. Tragically however, he was struck by a fatal illness, leaving his two wives without children. Hastinapura was lost and without a ruler. Due to his vow, Bhishma refused to ascend the throne and so there was no heir. Without a successor, the immense Kuru dynasty would be brought to an end. In desperation, Satyavati summoned her first-born son. Long before she met Shantanu, she had an encounter with the great sage Parashara. Their union produced a child, the great sage Vyasa. As soon as he was born, he began developing into an adult of his own will. He promised his mother that whenever she needed him, he would be there.

If ever there was such a time, it was now. Satyavati thought of him and immediately he appeared. Eager to have a ruler, she urged her son to grant children to the two widowed queens. Vyasa was willing but cautioned his mother that it would be difficult for them to withstand his terrifying, unkempt appearance. That night he came before the first queen, Ambika. Filled with fright at his ghastly form, she covered her eyes and as a result, gave birth to the blind son, Dhritarashtra. The second queen, Ambalika, was also gripped by fear. She turned pale white and gave birth to Pandu who was of the same complexion. Dissatisfied with the outcome, Vyasa was persuaded by his mother to return to Ambika once again. The queen was petrified and could not face him, so she sent her maid servant to receive him. She waited on him with reverence and received a son, Vidura, who was to be the wisest of men.

Despite being the eldest, Dhritarashtra's blindness disqualified him to rule and so it was Pandu who was made king. Soon afterwards, Bhishma arranged for their marriages. Gandhari the princess of Gandhara had been blessed with a boon to have a hundred sons and seemed a good match for Dhritarashtra. Her father was reluctant to give his daughter to a blind prince. But under some pressure, he gave in. Her brother, Shakuni, was infuriated by the proposal. It was a disgrace to marry his sister to such a man. Regardless of his illustrious family, a prince who could not see was not qualified to marry his sister. The insult cut deep and it changed him forever. The impact of the whole affair gave Shakuni a new goal that was to define the rest of his life.

Gandhari Marries and Gives Birth to Duryodhana

Gandhari had no say in the matter, and right up

until the last hour she was oblivious to the fact that her husband was blind. When the news reached her, she was dumbfounded. Her dreams had been shattered, and in response she took a drastic decision. Gathering a cloth, she tied it over her eyes. If her husband could not see, then she too would live out her days in darkness. This was her gesture of love and respect towards him.

Meanwhile Pandu was married to two queens Kunti and Madri. He ruled well and conquered different lands. One fateful day whilst hunting, he shot a deer engaged in mating. This was no ordinary animal, it was a sage and his wife in disguise. With his dying words the sage cursed Pandu that because he had been slaughtered in the act of love, he too would lose his life the moment he touched his wife with desire. It was a terrible blow to the king. How could he rule with this curse hanging over him? Now there was no chance of producing an heir, and so from that moment he renounced the throne and chose to live in the forest with his wives.

Dhritarashtra became king and as time marched on, Gandhari became pregnant. But after a year had passed, there was still no sign of a child. It was at this time in the forest that Kunti revealed something extraordinary. Long ago she had been given a special mantra in which she could call upon any god to give her a child. Pandu could hardly contain his joy, he urged her to use it without delay. The first deity she invoked was dharma, who gave her a son named Yudhishthira. He was the embodiment of righteousness and would be renowned for his unflinching virtue. Next Kunti called upon Vayu, the god of wind, and received a son, Bhima who was born with unparalleled strength. Then Indra was summoned and he blessed them with Arjuna. He would be famed throughout the world as the greatest of warriors. The heavens resounded with all manner of glorifications; this child would change history and would display unprecedented valour.

The same mantra was given to Madri who appealed to the Ashvin twins, the gods of health and medicine. She received twins, Nakula and Sahadeva, who would be celebrated for their beauty and knowledge. Together these five sons born of celestial deities became known as the Pandavas.

When Gandhari heard about the birth of Yudhishthira, she cursed fate. It had been nearly two years and still there was no sign of any child. She had been promised a hundred sons, but she did not even have one. In anger she struck herself with tremendous force and delivered a lump of flesh as hard as an iron ball. Gandhari and all her servants were horrified at what they saw. Arrangements were made to dispose of it, and at that moment Vyasa appeared. He divided up the mass into a hundred and one pieces and placed them into ghee pots. In due course, they heard a child braying like a donkey from one of the containers.

Immediately evil omens were seen everywhere. Wolves, jackals and vultures could be heard, while fires and winds ravaged the land. Vidura warned Dhritarashtra that this child would be the ruin of the whole dynasty, so he pleaded with him to cast the baby aside and save his race. The blind king, who was elated at the birth of his son refused to listen, his attachment to his first born, Duryodhana, had already set too deep. In total, Gandhari and her husband begot one daughter and a hundred sons known as the Kauravas.

Pandu and his wives were still in the forest. But one unfortunate day, the spring season stirred his senses. In a fit of desire, he approached Madri and at once collapsed dead. The wives lamented their loss, but the guilt Madri felt compelled her to enter the funeral pyre with her dead husband. The five sons were left alone with Kunti, and under the instruction of the sages, they made the journey back to the kingdom of Hastinapura. Now the stage was set for the great feud between the Kauravas and Pandavas to begin.

Duryodhana's Hatred for the Pandavas Begins

Right from the outset, Duryodhana could not stand the presence of his cousins. He spent his time plotting and planning ways to eliminate them. He had a particular hatred for Bhima who routinely teased and playfully assaulted the Kaurava brothers. The rivalry consumed Duryodhana, so much so, that he poisoned Bhima and dumped his body in the river. Astoundingly, Bhima returned stronger and mightier than ever. Duryodhana knew he had to wait. When the tide was in his favour, he would strike and destroy his enemies. There was no way he would allow Yudhishthira to take the kingdom which belonged to him.

As time passed the princes learnt the use of weapons from the great sage Drona. Once they were of age, the time came for them to display their talent to the citizens of Hastinapura. In a packed arena they showed all they had learned. Arjuna stood head and shoulders above the rest. He had mastered the use of divine weapons and exhibited every quality of a warrior to perfection. The crowd roared in approval and all the while Duryodhana looked on with jealousy and anxiety. Then, the whole mood was disrupted as a radiant young man entered. His armour and earrings were shining resplendently. Fearlessly, he called upon all those present to witness his skill; the people marvelled at what he could do. Everyone wondered who this person was and where he came from. There was, however, one person who instantly recognised him.

Kunti was as honest and pious a woman as you could find, yet she held a secret which haunted her. Long ago when she first received the mantra to have children, she doubted its power. In order to test it, she looked up at Surya, the sun god and invoked his presence. Immediately he appeared and offered her a son. Kunti was shocked and protested that she did not want a child. She was a maiden and unmarried, and there was no way she could accept him. Surya however, was bound by the mantra and so against her wishes she was given a son. The prospect of being a mother filled her with fear. How could she keep him? She would be shamed by her family and society. With tears and regret she placed him in a basket and sent him down the river. That was the last she saw of him, and now her son Karna stood captivating the crowd with his skill.

He wanted to show he was the best of warriors and to do this he had to defeat Arjuna. He openly challenged him to a duel, but fate had other ideas. Kripa, the head priest, intervened. "Princes should only fight with equals," he declared. The elders demanded to know who Karna's parents were. This lone warrior stuttered and looked to the ground in shame. He was the adopted son of a charioteer and had no qualification to engage in warfare. The crowd began murmuring amongst themselves, people began jeering and uttering insults at this low-born person who had dared to enter the royal arena. The humiliation was palpable. At that key moment, Duryodhana stepped in. He rebuked the elders and the heckling mob. He demanded to know why somebody's status should have any bearing on their right to fight. Rallying against the Pandavas, he sat Karna down and there on that very spot anointed him king of Anga. Karna would never forget this act. For this one gesture, he pledged a lifetime of unwavering friendship. Duryodhana smiled, for he had won the most powerful of allies.

The Pandavas Marry Draupadi

Time moved on and the Pandavas were formidable in strength and virtue. They conquered enemies and won the hearts of the citizens. Dhritarashtra was distressed, as was Duryodhana. If Yudhishthira was named king, then the Kauravas would be second-class servants. They would lose all their power and authority. With Dhritarashtra's permission Duryodhana hatched a plan. The Pandavas were ordered to attend a festival in Varnavat. A house was specifically built with all kinds of flammable material. In the middle of the night, while the Pandavas and Kunti slept, it was set on fire. Fortunately, Vidura had warned them of Duryodhana's plans and they were able to escape. To everyone else however, it looked like the brothers had died. News of their apparent death reached Hastinapura and the whole kingdom was plunged into grief.

Little did they know that the Pandavas were living out their lives disguised as sages. Keeping a low profile, they stayed in the house of a family in a nearby village. Word eventually reached them about a contest to win the hand of Draupadi, the princess of Panchala. She was born from fire, dark in complexion and matchless in beauty. All the kings were aching to wed her, but none of them could pass the test of archery. After they had all failed, Arjuna stepped forward. Disguised as he was, nobody in the congregation recognised him, apart from one person, Lord Krishna. He silently watched as Arjuna strung the bow and successfully performed the task. Draupadi had been won and as fate had determined from her previous birth, she became the wife of all five Pandavas.

The marriage of Draupadi to the Pandavas reached the ears of Dhritarashtra. Outwardly he was elated and full of joy that they were still alive. Behind closed doors however, he feared for Duryodhana's inheritance. He had no choice but to invite them back, but instead of offering them the kingdom that was rightfully theirs, he divided it up and offered them the dry barren land of Khandavaprastha. This was clearly unfair. It was a vast stretch of land which had nothing of value. Yudhishthira did not protest but gracefully accepted it. With the help of Krishna by his side, the Pandavas ended up building the greatest of all kingdoms. Their palace was filled with stunning architecture and was bedecked with jewels. Through various conquests, they had accumulated unimaginable wealth. They had won the hearts of the people and their kingdom was renamed Indraprastha, a veritable heaven on Earth. In order to increase their glory, they performed the great ceremony known as the Rajasuya sacrifice. All the kings in all the lands came to pledge their loyalty to Yudhishthira. Duryodhana was one of them. It pained him to see the success of his cousins. He was burning with envy, and something had to be done.

Shakuni Robs and Disgraces the Pandavas

Utterly demoralised he ran to Shakuni for a solution. His uncle was not known for his skill in war, but he was a master tactician. The Pandavas took their counsel from Krishna and followed His every word whereas Duryodhana relied on Shakuni. His deceitful and sharp intelligence was always searching for ways to empower his nephew. Rather than risk open war, he proposed that Yudhishthira be invited for a gambling match. Shakuni would play for Duryodhana and win all the wealth of the Pandavas. Both of them pressed Dhritarashtra for approval. Being fearful of Vidura and Bhishma he initially refused. But Duryodhana stood his ground. He shouted and stamped his feet, and eventually the king caved in.

Even though he suspected a trap, out of respect, Yudhishthira could never refuse an invitation from an elder. Along with his brothers and Draupadi, they came to Hastinapura. Everybody assembled for the gambling match. Shakuni knew this was his time to shine. The dice he had was loaded and would obey his every command, so there was no way he could lose. It started innocently enough. There were simple wagers of jewellery; then chariots and horses were bet, next elephants, maids and soldiers were all laid down. Throw after throw Shakuni won. Little by little Yudhishthira was being robbed of all his assets. Duryodhana was elated. Yudhishthira carried on playing and every time the stakes were raised. Eventually he lost all his wealth and indeed his whole kingdom. Vidura pleaded with Dhritarashtra to end the game, but he was quickly shouted down by Duryodhana. Then the match took a new turn for the worse. With nothing else to gamble Yudhishthira offered Nakula, then Sahadeva, Arjuna and then finally Bhima. He lost all his brothers, yet he carried on and even lost himself. Duryodhana had won - he had defeated his enemies and the Pandavas were now his slaves. There was however, still one more prize to wager, Draupadi.

Everyone gasped in horror as Shakuni won yet again. Word was sent to bring Draupadi from her chambers, but she refused to come. Duryodhana was in no mood to tolerate disobedience. Enraged, he sent his brother, Dushasana, to demand she come immediately. Like a well-trained animal he wasted no time. Bursting into her apartment, he beat her and grabbed her by the hair. Dragging her through the palace he brought Draupadi into the assembly and threw her down. Duryodhana was ecstatic. He taunted her by slapping his thigh and telling her to come and sit on it.

The Pandavas were ordered to remove their clothes and then to everyone's horror the same was demanded of Draupadi. As Dushasana chased her all around the hall, she appealed to Bhishma, Drona, Kripa and the king but nobody could bring themselves to intervene. Despite the terrible abuse, they concluded that she had been 'fairly' won. This was dharma, they said and they could not bring themselves to transgress it. Wasting no time, Dushasana chased Draupadi around the hall and finally grabbed her sari.

After all her effort she gave up any hope of protecting herself and appealed to her one and only saviour, Krishna. Before everyone's eyes her prayers gave birth to a miracle. An endless supply of cloth manifested from nowhere, with all kinds of colours and silks. Dushasana kept pulling, but the sari never ran out. Exhausted, he collapsed and Draupadi's dignity was saved.

Gandhari was alarmed and pacified Draupadi as best she could. She was terrified that the anger of this woman would unleash a curse on her son. Dhritarashtra also rushed in to appease her. He offered her husbands their freedom and gave back their kingdom. He pathetically pleaded with Yudhishthira to forget this whole horrid affair. The Pandavas left, but Duryodhana would not relent. He had been robbed of victory and he could not let this lie. He pressed his father to call them back for a second game. Gandhari warned Dhritarashtra that the Kuru family would be destroyed if this saga continued. The blind king listened but was enslaved to the desires of his son.

The Pandavas were recalled. This time the game was simple: there would be one wager and the loser would retire to the forest for twelve years, spending one extra year in hiding. If they survived this, their kingdom would be returned to them. Yudhishthira yet again agreed, and as expected Shakuni won. Without a single drop of blood being spilled, Duryodhana's uncle had managed to defeat the mighty Pandavas.

Krishna Takes the Side of the Pandavas

The five brothers spent the years in exile and eventually time came for them to return. Not surprisingly, Duryodhana refused to give back their kingdom and so preparations for war began. The various kings in the land were approached by the two sides. Out of all of them, there was only one person who could guarantee victory and that was Krishna. Everyone knew of His strength and skill, but above all, His army was unstoppable. Arjuna had already set out to Dwaraka and Duryodhana was keen to get there first. Both arrived while Krishna was asleep, and they waited patiently by His bed eager to present their cases.

As soon as He awoke, Duryodhana demanded that Krishna join the Kauravas. In reply, Krishna declared that He would not fight in this war. To one side He would give His illustrious army, to the other, He would be with them but unarmed. Arjuna was given first choice and did not hesitate to choose Krishna. Duryodhana was quietly overjoyed and gleefully accepted the army. After all, what use was Krishna if He was unwilling to fight?

Fearing the might of the Pandavas, Dhritarashtra sent his trusted servant Sanjaya to urge Yudhishthira to give up on this war. He lectured him on detachment and told him to renounce the idea of ruling the kingdom. Under the guise of righteousness, he was desperately trying to save his son. In response, Krishna placed Himself forward to go to Hastinapura and try one last time for peace. In front of the entire assembly, Krishna attempted to persuade Duryodhana to see sense. Bhishma said his piece in support, as did Gandhari, but none of it moved him even an inch. Frustrated at the torrent of opposition, Duryodhana organised a plan to take Krishna prisoner. It was at this point that the Lord showed the whole courtroom His cosmic form. The Kauravas and even Dhritarashtra saw the different deities, and celestial beings in His body.

The whole assembly was stunned at this divine vision. Everybody bowed their heads in awe. Even then Duryodhana was not swayed, he passed the whole thing off as a conjuring trick. Having failed to capture Krishna, he stormed out with his uncle and brothers. Vidura tried one final time to make Dhritarashtra see sense, but Duryodhana caught wind of his words. There was no way he was going to allow the son of a maid to poison his father's mind. He hurled a barrage of insults. They wounded Vidura and enough was enough. The minister who had spent his whole life in service to the kingdom, finally stormed out of the palace. There was no doubt now, the war was inevitable.

Before Krishna returned to the Pandavas he met with Karna. He revealed to him for the first time the truth of his birth. Karna was no charioteer's son, he was a warrior of royal blood. He was born as the eldest son of Kunti and brother to the Pandavas. Krishna offered him a way out of the Kaurava camp. Now was the time to claim his rightful place with Yudhishthira. He could rule the world and alongside him Krishna would be his ally. His words, however, did not move Karna. In fact, nothing could take him from the side of Duryodhana. His friendship was more important than wealth, power and even Krishna Himself. Even though he knew the Kauravas would lose, he would not change course.

The Great War Begins

Almost every warrior, prince and king descended upon the Kurukshetra battlefield. The Kaurava army outnumbered the Pandavas and Bhishma was in command. He loved the Pandavas dearly and he consistently condemned Duryodhana's behaviour throughout. But he was a Kuru, and so his loyalty was always to the throne of Hastinapura. This, in his eyes, was dharma. On the other side stood Arjuna in his chariot driven by Krishna. As the conches were blown, he asked his dear friend to take him between the two armies. There Arjuna scanned his family, friends and many well-wishers. Seeing so many of his loved ones on the opposing side, he was overcome with emotion. "How could it have come to this?" he wondered. No matter how bad Duryodhana was, it could not be right to kill your own family; surely this runs against righteousness. He broke down and pleaded to Krishna for guidance.

Thus began the greatest of all conversations. Krishna instructed him on the nature of the soul and the truth of

Himself as the Supreme Lord. Upon Arjuna's request He revealed His universal form in which all of creation could be seen. Arjuna saw worlds being made and destroyed. Past, present and future were all there. Victory for the Pandavas and the death of the Kauravas had already happened - Krishna had already decided the outcome of the war. All the while Sanjaya, who had been blessed with divine vision, was narrating everything to Dhritarashtra in the palace. The king was trembling in fear. He knew that one by one his sons would be slaughtered. It was only a matter of time before he lost everything.

The fighting began and with Bhishma leading the way, the Kauravas had the upper hand. He seemed impenetrable; even Arjuna was unable to drive him back. At one point, Krishna grew so frustrated that he picked up his chariot wheel and rushed to attack Bhishma. The old grandfather threw down his weapons, he was overjoyed to behold Krishna's fury. This was the Supreme Lord and there would be nothing greater than to die at His hands. But at the last minute, Arjuna intervened and calmed Krishna's rage.

Days passed and Bhishma looked more invincible. Exasperated at the destruction of their soldiers, the Pandavas approached him after sunset and humbly asked how he could be defeated. Bhishma told them there was only one warrior he would not fight and that was Shikhandi.

In his previous life Shikhandi had been Amba, the sister of Ambika and Ambalika. She had already pledged her heart to another king when Bhishma took her and her sisters away to be married to his brother. When he learned of this, Bhishma allowed her to go back to him. But out of pride Amba's lover refused to accept her. Having been rejected, she demanded Bhishma marry her, because after all, had he not taken her away, she would already be married. Because of his oath, this was simply not an option. Feeling dishonored and utterly abandoned, she sought vengeance against Bhishma. All she wanted was his death. Knowing it could not be fulfilled in this life, she threw her body into fire and was reborn as Shikhandi. In Bhishma's eyes 'he' would always be Amba, a woman and so he refused to raise his bow against her. The Pandavas knew what needed to be done.

The next day Shikhandi challenged Bhishma, and as stated he refused to take up his weapons. Seizing the opportunity, Arjuna stood behind Shikhandi and began firing arrows. Bhishma was covered in blood and the onslaught finally made him collapse. He lay above the ground supported by the very arrows which had pierced his body. All the warriors stopped their battles and the war temporarily ceased. Both the Kauravas and the Pandavas gathered to revere this great hero who had brought them up and dedicated his whole life to the throne of Hastinapura.

Drona was next in command for the Kauravas. It was under his watch that the dear son of Arjuna, Abhimanyu, was brutally and unfairly killed. After he was defeated, Karna took control. All he had ever wanted was to be recognised as the greatest of all warriors and now was his chance. Throughout his life he had been famed for his generosity; whatever anyone asked of him, he was ready to give. No sacrifice was too much. Even for Duryodhana he was ready to give his life for their friendship. Thanks to him, finally the day had arrived where he would face Arjuna as his equal.

The battle was fierce and unlike any other. Both were experts in invoking celestial weapons. They were evenly matched until suddenly the chariot wheel of Karna was caught in the ground. Under the rules of war, he was allowed time to free it. Arjuna dutifully waited, but then Krishna began reminding him of the injustices he and his brothers had suffered. His son, Abhimanyu, had been wrongfully ambushed, and they had been deceived and abused in the game of dice, so now was not the time to hold onto rules. Goaded by Krishna's sharp words, Arjuna took the opportunity and killed Karna.

Duryodhana Is Slain

The Kauravas were decimated. Bhima had killed ninety-nine brothers, Sahadeva had defeated Shakuni. Duryodhana was all alone. With no army and few allies, the war looked as good as over. Gandhari had produced a hundred sons and now she had just one. She had lived a dutiful and pious life, yet all she had experienced was tragedy. The pain and grief were unbearable. She could not be left childless, and had to take action.

Gandhari called her son, Duryodhana, and instructed him to come to her completely naked. She would give him a blessing which would protect his body from any assault. He did as he was asked, but while walking to his mother's quarters it just so happened that Krishna was passing by. He laughed at Duryodhana. How could a grown man come to his mother in this state? At least, He argued, he should cover his waist. Somewhat embarrassed, Duryodhana took some leaves to retain his modesty and went to Gandhari. For the first time since she swore never to see light again all those years ago, she took off her blindfold and gazed at her son. All the power from her austerities and spiritual practice were showered on Duryodhana. There was just one problem; he had covered himself below the waist, this area would still be vulnerable. Gandhari knew that fate wanted her son dead.

The Pandavas sought out Duryodhana to end the war once and for all. Bhima was set to fight him in a mace duel. They ferociously beat one another; sparks flew in the air as their clubs collided. Duryodhana, protected by his mother's blessing, looked unstoppable. Under Krishna's instruction, Bhima knew that although it was against the rules, he had to strike below the waist. The next time Duryodhana leapt into the air, Bhima's mace came crashing down on his thigh, that same thigh which Duryodhana had asked Draupadi to sit on in the gambling hall. He plummeted down to the ground and there this mighty prince was left alone writhing in agony, bleeding to death. The war was over and finally the Pandavas could claim back the kingdom.

Rivers of blood and endless corpses lay on the battlefield. All the women descended to identify and find their dead loved ones. Gandhari was amongst them and finally she came to Duryodhana. The Pandavas and Krishna approached her, as she wailed pitifully. She could no longer hide her true feelings; she knew this colossal tragedy could have been prevented. If Krishna was God, He could have stopped the war. Gandhari's bitterness erupted into a curse. Krishna's family would also suffer the same fate as the Kurus; they would annihilate themselves and their women would suffer as she did.

Yudhishthira was crowned king, but the many deaths and turmoil of the great war remained with him. He found no peace of mind and was greatly perturbed. Krishna told him that Bhishma was waiting for an auspicious time to leave his body. He was still lying on the battlefield but was about to depart. Now was the time to gain all the priceless knowledge from this great soul. The Pandavas and Krishna gathered around him. Day after day, they received wisdom on every aspect of life. Then when the sun began its journey northwards and with the permission of Krishna, Bhishma summoned death and ascended to heaven.

After some time of Yudhishthira ruling the kingdom, Dhritarashtra and Gandhari realised it was time to turn their attention to the world beyond. Along with Sanjaya they retired to the forest to perform austerities. The curse that Krishna had incurred, soon took effect. After a drunken dispute, His entire Yadava clan destroyed one another. Leaving the bloodshed and chaos behind, Krishna found an isolated spot and rested. A hunter, mistaking His foot for a deer, released an arrow. It was the excuse Krishna needed. The Lord who had fulfilled the mission for which He came, finally returned to His Supreme abode.

Krishna Comes as the Master to Expose the Ego

Within the Mahabharata, Krishna is the Supreme Lord, the descent of God on Earth. Throughout the story, the secret of His incarnation remains largely hidden. Apart from a handful of people, most dismiss Him as a powerful but ordinary king of the Yadava race. He is respected as a great hero, a friend to the righteous Pandava brothers and an expert strategist, but only a few have the eyes to perceive His cosmic will at work. The others do not see, how step by step, He is organising the build-up to the war. All the great and arrogant warriors of the world are being summoned to the battlefield to be destroyed.

Like Krishna, the Master is the personification of Divine wisdom. Sometimes He speaks to us from within, sometimes through life circumstances and sometimes He comes in the form of a Person. In all situations the Master manifests to correct and uplift us.

Just as Krishna dictates the great war, He also exposes the ego and ushers all its allies to the surface. The Master is full of Love and has the grace to remove everything holding us back. Eventually, He sees to it that all weeds are pulled, and every ounce of insincerity is eliminated.

Duryodhana is the reason for this terrible war. In his arrogance, he refuses to yield the kingdom to the Pandavas. Those who have taken his side, not only stand against the Pandavas, they stand opposed to Krishna too. In the same way, this epic war is playing out before us. Duryodhana stands for the part of us seeking selfish enjoyment; the part of us which lures us away from who we truly are.

While the characters supporting Duryodhana claim to be following righteousness, somehow, they have found themselves ready to fight against Krishna. Even though Bhishma, Karna, and even Gandhari have many redeeming qualities, they are on the wrong side serving the Kauravas.

This is how hypocrisy works. The ego is at its strongest when it uses virtue against Truth. Because of their loyalty to Duryodhana, they can no longer be seen as righteous – they are enemies that have to be defeated. They are different forms of negativity. To reveal our true connection with the Divine, Krishna comes as the Master to eliminate them.

The characters described in the following pages shine a light on the ego and the various psychological patterns it hides behind. Once we understand their thoughts and behaviour, we have a profound tool to self-analyse. We can spot the ego's stages of growth and develop the necessary discrimination to see when we are falling under its control.

In the following pages, we shall analyse the different characters and unveil the various states of hypocrisy.

The ensuing six chapters are based on key personalities:

- **Duryodhana** is the hypocrisy of self-gratification. We enter the spiritual path believing we are searching for something higher, but the ego makes us use every person, and situation, including the Master for our own selfish pleasure.

- **Dhritarashtra** is the hypocrisy that refuses responsibility. When faced with the need to change, the ego keeps us in denial. We create all kinds of justifications to avoid doing what is necessary for our path.

- **Gandhari** is the hypocrisy of resentment. In an effort to be good, we suppress various desires. This sacrifice allows the ego to create a sense of victimhood. Eventually our rage turns into vengeance against the Master.

- **Shakuni** is the hypocrisy of cunningness. The need to be recognised makes us strategically manipulate people and spiritual ideas. The ego creates a duplicitous persona that competes with others for attention.

- **Bhishma** is the hypocrisy of dogmatism. We are afraid of going astray and so we become obsessed with tradition and rules. The ego enjoys being righteous and makes us overly disciplined. We lose perspective and miss the point of walking a spiritual path.

- **Karna** is the hypocrisy of false compassion. We believe that moral values and feelings are more important than Truth. The ego exploits this misunderstanding and uses kindness as a virtuous front to have its way.

After describing the different faces of the ego, the final chapter offers a way out of the maze of self-deceit. When **Draupadi**, the wife of the Pandavas, is tormented by the Kauravas, she turns to Krishna in desperation. This act of helplessness is what disentangles us from the ego's clutches. Step by step, we are lifted out of delusion and brought back to grace. The state of surrender opens the gates of heaven and allows us to feel the presence of the Divine.

These chapters illustrate the vast spectrum of spiritual hypocrisy. It is often the case that what we need to know most, is what we would like to know least. But if we are striving to be as authentic as we can be, we must always be ready, if not eager, to look at what needs to be changed. We all have a degree of sincerity and when we live from it, facing the ego is not a bold effort but a natural instinct. This book is an attempt to nurture that instinct. It is a tool designed to help us identify the inner work we all need to do.

The Love of the Divine is not as far away as we think, It is there, waiting for us. By going through the following chapters we can start to experience it. We can rise above the games of the ego and come back to a place of innocence and simplicity.

Duryodhana – The Hypocrisy of Self-Gratification

He looked down at his leg. Blood was still pouring out of the gaping wound and the pain was making him delirious. This great prince of the Kuru dynasty who was once surrounded by servants and ministers, who could not want for anything, lay alone in the dark forest. Struggling for breath, he could feel that life was ebbing away from his body.

As if compelled by some unknown force, Duryodhana began replaying events from his life. He remembered the rage at the first meeting with his cousins. From the outset, he never saw them as family, they were a threat, enemies that had to be eliminated. No matter what the cost, Duryodhana would never bow to them. Their pain was his joy. The envy he had was overwhelming. It was responsible for everything, for the slaughter of millions of men. It was the reason he was lying there that night.

He cast his mind back to the arena when all the Kuru princes were displaying their talents for the first time. He remembered the anxiety as he watched Arjuna dazzle the crowd. He had never seen such power and skill before. How could the Pandavas possibly be defeated? No one in the Kaurava camp could match him. But then fate gifted a solution. The moment Karna stormed the stadium, he could feel the tide

was changing. Here was someone who could defeat Arjuna and carry him to victory. Karna's vulnerability was an opportunity. By rescuing him from humiliation he had won a friend for life.

His thoughts passed to his blind father Dhritarashtra. He was a pathetic old man. Duryodhana knew which strings to pull, he knew what would eventually make him crack. His righteous exterior was just a veil; ultimately, his father wanted him on the throne. The other elders had influence, but Dhritarashtra ruled and as long as he was on side, they had no say. Even Bhishma and Vidura could not intervene. Whether it was trying to burn the Pandavas alive or challenging his cousins to war, the blind king was always ready to do his bidding. Duryodhana knew how to turn him away from his conscience.

He looked back at the game of dice and mourned how close he was to victory. His uncle, Shakuni, had given him everything on a plate. The Pandavas were his slaves and nobody could contest him. Bhishma, Drona and Kripa had to stay silent. He felt liberated. Finally, he had the freedom to unleash all his venom. Draupadi was his property, and were it not for that miraculous event, he would have disgraced her in front of everybody.

Then there was Krishna. That fateful day in Dwaraka was the turning point. Duryodhana remembered how he and Arjuna stood awaiting His decision. Which side would He choose to fight on? Krishna put His offer on the table: Either choose His immense army, the finest in the land, or choose Himself, unarmed and unwilling to fight. When Arjuna rejected the army and chose Krishna, Duryodhana nearly erupted into laughter. It looked like an unprecedented moment of madness. Now he realised, that was the decision which cost him the kingdom. Soon after, that same Krishna came as a peace ambassador on behalf of the Pandavas. Every word He uttered infuriated Duryodhana. Who did He think He was coming into the king's court making vain threats? In a fit of rage, he ordered Krishna to be taken prisoner. It was then that the Lord shocked the assembly and revealed His blinding cosmic form. To any sane person, that would have been enough to avoid war. Somehow Duryodhana managed to dismiss the whole event. Everyone but him knew the truth, that the Kauravas were doomed.

Now as he lay there in his own blood-soaked garments,

it began to dawn on him that despite having the largest army, despite having the greatest warriors fighting for him, he didn't have Krishna, and without Krishna he had lost everything.

Duryodhana – The Ego that Uses and Abuses[2]

Duryodhana has a warped and twisted view of dharma. He believes that his highest purpose is not to be righteous and serve, but to defeat his enemies and fulfil his desires. For him, life is about destroying all those who stand in his way through any means necessary. He believes we should live by the law of the jungle, where only the strongest deserve to survive. The desire to sit on the throne of Hastinapura and vanquish the Pandavas consumes him. Everything and everyone is a utility to be exploited for this end. When Karna stands vulnerable and humiliated, Duryodhana seizes the opportunity to strike an alliance that serves him. When Dhritarashtra displays weakness, he is happy to use his father's attachment to get his way. For Duryodhana it doesn't matter who suffers and it doesn't matter whose life is ruined.

Duryodhana stands for the rawest form of the ego. This ego wants to win, to dominate and conquer everything around it. It has no interest in serving something higher. It wants to transform us into primitive beings that seek pleasure and enjoyment. In the beginning almost everybody who walks a spiritual path has a degree of sincerity. We want to find something the world cannot offer. Deep down we know that we have a purpose and

[2] Paramahamsa Vishwananda, Bhagavad Gita, page 32.

we long to discover what that is. Without realising it however, we can easily develop attractions to other things that this path offers. We can form new relationships, there are chances to learn and opportunities to express our talents. Although these can make us grow, if we are not vigilant, they can also take our minds away from inner development. Instead of focusing on a higher goal, we can become motivated by whatever satisfies our selfish interests. Unconsciously we start looking not for what will make us transform, but simply for what we like. If we are not careful, the determination to change and evolve can gradually get put to one side.

When we are sincere, there is maturity. We feel the calling from within and are willing to take responsibility for it. At some level, there is an understanding that our life is not our own and is meant for something higher. But just as Duryodhana wishes to eliminate the Pandavas and rule the kingdom, the ego is out to oppress the qualities that build our relationship with the Divine. It makes us look for 'feel good' spirituality that gives quick results.

At the start of our journey when everything is fresh and new, it is natural to have a lot of enthusiasm. Everything is exciting and we want to absorb as much as we can. On the outside at least, we can seem like a dedicated seeker. We are eager to get involved and learn new things. However, when we are controlled by the ego, it is not the desire for inner change that inspires us, it is the craving for some kind of gratification. We are not interested in serving or living for a grander purpose. There is a hunger for enjoyment and the spiritual path is used to satisfy it.

Duryodhana's desire to conquer is fundamentally the ego's attempt to gain power. It is where we try to make the world and others conform to our expectations. We have our ideas, our vision of how things should be and we uncompromisingly attempt to make everything around us bow down to it. Often when we do not get our way, we either quickly move onto something else or we rebel. The ego wants freedom. It does not want to be constricted or told what to do.

The spiritual path is also looking to give us freedom, but not some cheap version that gives material happiness. It is looking to deliver a state where we rise above any attachment to the people and things around us. It is where we know ourselves as the soul. This freedom involves a process. It is about sacrificing certain things and committing ourselves. It takes time and effort, all of which are in opposition to the ego's agenda.

The Ego Makes Us Superficial and Unable to Commit to the Spiritual Path

Duryodhana mistakes his determined arrogance with being a righteous warrior. He is fearless and will do anything to destroy his enemies. Instead of being weak and giving in, he is ready to risk his life in war. In the same way the ego has a way of making us mistake our pleasure-seeking attitude with devotion to our goal.

Because sincerely seeking the Divine involves being eager and earnest, we can easily believe there is something sacred in the way we run after spiritual practices and activities. This kind of excitement however, has little to do with devotion and is actually a form of lust.

Lust does not simply mean sexual gratification; it is any enjoyment the ego derives. If we have real devotion, we patiently want to satisfy the deep calling of our soul. We are willing to play the long game. We know that transformation will take time and involves significant commitment. Lust, however, has no patience. Instead of waiting and receiving, it looks to grab and take what it can. The ego has no time to waste; it wants instant results with no effort. This attitude makes us restless and shallow. It stops us having the willingness to discover something meaningful. Like a child at the playground, the spiritual path becomes more like a game we play for fun.

The ego brings a mindset where we underestimate the level of commitment that is needed on our path. Words like 'surrender' and 'self-realisation' are not life changing goals to strive for, but trivial concepts that we can casually talk about. Rather than spirituality being a road to transcendence, the ego transforms it into a marketplace. It is not a path, but rather a series of stalls and shops with different items to choose from. There are so many things being offered. Practices, philosophies, communities and organisations are all available for us to sample. We become like a customer who wants to try on the dresses and jewellery. The ego makes us thirsty for new techniques with exciting results.

Instead of finding inspiration by going deep into one thing, we are constantly jumping around looking to take what we can. Once we have received what we want, we quickly become bored and march on to the next thing without looking back. Like a restless addict, the ego is always looking for its next fix. It wants the shortest possible route for the biggest possible reward. Far from being a goal, spiritual progress endangers everything the ego is out to achieve. The last thing it desires is transformation. Real change is the letting go of self-centred intentions, it is gaining a grander perspective and becoming more humble. For the ego, a shift closer to the Divine is a threat, not a blessing. It is something to be feared, not welcomed.

Spiritual practices and movements not only alleviate our boredom but provide a wonderful sense of entertainment. Listening to talk of past lives, learning about other planes of existence, experimenting with energies and inward states of consciousness can all give us the feeling that we are onto something, that we know things the rest of the world has yet to catch up on. The feeling of being on a search for Truth is exciting. We can become addicted to reading great pearls of wisdom and marvelling at profound insights of different speakers. The ego wants to keep us in this state. The more we run after entertainment, the more we shy away from real inner work. We get stuck in believing we are evolving, without actually evolving. In our minds the fantasy of spiritual growth is more enticing than the reality.

Inevitably there is little respect for rules and disciplines. Traditions with specific philosophies and practices can all be twisted and readapted to whatever suits us. The ego convinces us to freestyle things. There is no need to follow regulations and customs; we can just go with whatever feels good. Rather than look for meaningful change within, we run after experiences that give 'energy' highs. Chasing states of consciousness and other esoteric ideas are particularly appealing. We might believe we are advancing, but often there is no real aim to what we are doing. The ego stops us having the commitment needed to make any progress. Its superficial attitude prevents us from going deep enough to sustain any real interest. As a result, highs come quickly and disappear even quicker.

The inability to commit to one situation is often a symptom of an inner disharmony. We are looking to escape who we are. For some reason, we are not at peace with ourselves. Perhaps we have a lack of love or confidence and so we try to divert our attention elsewhere. One week we are practising meditation, the next we are running to another form of yoga. We take initiation into one spiritual tradition and then a few months later we abandon it and move on to a different one. The ego only cares about gathering as many of these experiences as possible. It will do what it can to keep us engaged at the most superficial level. This is where we can find pleasure, we can do as we please, without having to change.

The Ego Blinds Us to the Wisdom of Life

Unlike Duryodhana, the Pandavas face their trials and find a deeper place of wisdom. Difficulties teach them to pin their hopes and desires on Krishna. Similarly, if we are sincere to our path, we see that challenges push us further within and open a space where we can grow. We understand that life and the situations we face are the language of the Divine. Everything that happens is a potential lesson. It is our higher purpose prompting and nudging us in the right direction. Duryodhana is oblivious to this. When things go well it is a victory, while difficulties only signal a major mishap. He is not looking to find some deeper perspective, he simply wants to win.

Likewise, for the ego, challenges are not profound opportunities, but interruptions to its satisfaction. As much as we might say everything happens for a reason, often there is little interest to find out what that reason is. The more our intentions are focused on grabbing what we want, the less scope we have to discover any real wisdom.

The ego makes us unaware and unable to decipher the truths we need to learn.

Whenever life shows us the way forward, we cannot see it. Even when the same lessons keep returning through different situations, we find a way of ignoring or reinterpreting them. Instead of pausing and reflecting on what we have to change, we try to power through. This is especially true when we are being denied something we desperately want. Rather than accept that our desire might not be best for us, we keep trying to force a way to make it happen. Despite knowing things would be so much easier if we let go and moved with the flow of life, we still cling on. We fear the consequences of change. The ego makes us focus on what we are losing but never on what we might gain. As a result we can end up being stubborn and insensitive to the insights being delivered to us.

Somehow we are tricked into believing we are searching for self realisation. But all we are doing is sustaining the deception of being a serious spiritual seeker whilst pursuing what we want.

Duryodhana Uses the Battlefield to Win a Kingdom – The Ego Uses the Spiritual Path to Fulfil Worldly Ambition

The spiritual path is like the Kurukshetra battlefield, it is a place where we fight and work things out. The kind of battle we engage in depends on our intentions. The Pandavas come to Kurukshetra, not to win a kingdom, but to finally establish dharma. Likewise, if we are a seeker, our mindset is fixed upon inner change. We leave behind the ambitions of the world to fulfil the longing of our soul. Unfortunately, the ego gives us a mindset which looks to satisfy materialistic ambitions. Instead of striving to connect with our higher nature, we try to attain what we could not get from the world.

When the job we took is not what we thought it would be, or when our relationships keep collapsing bringing nothing but misery, there is an emptiness that needs to be filled. The spiritual scene often has everything we are looking for, especially if we are part of an organisation or movement. Projects, events and positions can all be used to make up for our failed aspirations. There is potentially a whole new world in which we can redefine ourselves. Although the spiritual path may not be our first choice, because life has not delivered what we want, we can end up using it to reach the same goals we previously missed out on. Becoming 'spiritual' looks like we have renounced the world and risen above material desires. Real renunciation however is letting go of things even when we know we can have them, not because we have been rejected by them.

The trap we can fall into is that instead of using spirituality to awaken a Divine connection, we simply transfer our worldly desires into a spiritual context. Externally everything might seem different. It looks like we have a new aim and a new philosophy to live by, but in reality our ego wants the same things as any other materialistic person. It simply uses the spiritual path as an escape from a life that was already dissatisfying. By taking on a new spiritual identity we have the chance to run away from an old tired identity that was no longer serving us.

In the beginning, it feels like we are starting afresh, that we are 'born again'. We can leave behind all the wounds and issues from our past. We can move forward with a clean slate and reinvent ourselves. However, so long as the ego's desires are still there, all we end up doing is transferring old baggage from one house to another. The context has changed but the inner state has not.

When we are sincere to our path, we do not think in the same way as we did before. Success is defined purely by how much we are growing within. We are clear that mundane worldly aspirations cannot satisfy us. While it may be tempting to run after opportunities to fulfil some old desire, we know our life is so much more than this. As a result, we do not try to make up for what we missed out on. There is no need to use spirituality as a substitute for an old life that was not working. We have finished with it and now we want something higher. The spiritual path is not a career move, it is a chance to know our soul.

The Ego Is Searching for Power

One of the reasons we bring the world onto the spiritual path is that the ego needs to prove itself. It tries to make us show people the talent and expertise we have. Consequently, we are pushed to take up new roles and lead from the front. Instead of allowing things to happen by themselves, we try to go out and force things to happen. There is a desire to achieve, and also receive the credit for achieving. Without realising it, our intentions can move from trying to selflessly serve, to meeting our personal desires. We want our spiritual résumé to be impressive. The more events we can be part of, the more projects we can start up, the more we feel satisfied at our accomplishments.

Because of the ego's enthusiasm, our actions are often imbalanced and excessive. We unnecessarily go the extra mile when it is not needed and heroically perform tasks that are not required. Occasionally instead of helping we end up becoming a nuisance. The ego is not interested in the greater good nor is it concerned with the overall success of the tasks we are part of. The main aim is to be in the thick of things and be noticed by others.

When we belong to a group or spiritual organisation, we may go on the hunt for positions of authority. They are especially appealing because the ego gets to exercise control and make important decisions. In the world we were insignificant, but now in our new spiritual arena, our opinions matter. People have to listen, and we have real influence. The more responsibility our role demands the more the ego is appeased. We do not want to be that devotee in the background, who silently carries out work behind the scenes. There is no fun in being anonymous. The ego wants to have an active and prominent role. If possible, we desire a position where major decisions are made, where we get to control and influence a number of people. The ego loves being the gatekeeper that decides if someone can have what they want. We are the ones that get to approve or reject proposals.

This does not always have to manifest in positions of authority. We can develop a possessiveness over any kind of service we do. Even when we are given small tasks to perform, the ego marks its territory around our job. We may not be looking for praise and recognition, but because we are so identified with our work, we cling to it. This is especially true if we have been doing it for a long time. We do not want to give it up and allow someone else the chance to serve, nor do we want too many people interfering and telling us how to carry out our duty. The ego turns simple opportunities to serve, into projects that only we have the rights over. Power is addictive, and the ego constantly tries to find ways to get it.

In contrast, when we are sincere to our path, we rise past this pettiness. In every action and in every project, we are trying to bring forth what we carry within. Work becomes worship. We do not care who is doing what, we are not bothered whether the credit falls our way, we are just grateful for having the chance to be part of it. Our mind is always on what is for the greater good. We know the Divine is with us no matter what role we have. The whole plan of the ego is to try and rob us of this purity and make us the centre of all that happens.

Duryodhana Is Afraid of Losing the Kingdom – The Ego Makes Us Live in Insecurity

One of the consequences of being ruled by the ego is that we constantly live in fear. Even when Duryodhana has the kingdom, he is plagued with anxiety. As long as his enemies are alive, his position on the throne is in doubt. The ego makes us deeply insecure because everything it seeks is impermanent. Positions, respect, praise, and fame will all crumble at some point and intuitively we know this. At any moment somebody else may be placed onto centre stage, upstaging everything we have ever done. He or she may be wiser, more talented, or more devoted.

If, like Duryodhana, we are using the spiritual path to prop up material desires, then like Duryodhana we will not be able to rest. We will incessantly be worried about how we look in front of others, or whether we are the best at what we do. This anxiety can be exhausting but more importantly it makes us forget about the inner work that is needed. Rather than trying to selflessly offer something to others, we can end up spending most of our time strategizing how we can stay on top and maintain our reputation. The spiritual path becomes a political affair in which we tactically attempt to keep getting what we want.

Following the ego, can make us materially successful but spiritually we become a beggar. The lack of trust in life means that we have to scavenge for our place. Life is a war, in which we have to struggle and battle for what we want.

Even when we achieve our desires, we cannot guarantee holding onto them. The ego drags us into a place where nothing is assured.

If we have faith, we act responsibly and trust that whatever we need will be given to us. We know that whatever happens has been specifically designed for our growth. We are here to do our duty, but the rest is in the hands of the Divine. Instead of giving up fighting for what we want and trusting a higher plan, the ego makes us go it alone and deal with the consequences. We are led to believe that we are fully in control and sole masters of our destiny. The ego does not want us to accept what life has given us. It knows that surrendering to what is happening will mean letting go of our desires. It will mean embracing whatever life delivers. This runs against everything the ego stands for.

The Ego Uses Ungrounded Fantasy to Gain Pleasure

The ego of Duryodhana is looking for a short cut to enjoy and one such way is through ungrounded fantasy. By using delusional ideas, it fools us into believing we are making spiritual progress.

There is nothing wrong in turning to spirituality to fill a void in our life, but we can sometimes do this whilst pretending we seriously want to advance. Using spirituality to gain peace of mind or a sense of wellbeing is not the same as striving for self-realisation. As we dive into philosophy and ideas, it is easy to convince ourselves that we are serious spiritual seekers when we are not. In a short space of time we can move from someone who wants stress relief, to someone who believes they are an advanced yogi on a path to enlightenment. Quickly we can fall into the trap of believing we are ready and qualified to receive the highest states of realisation. The more intense we are, the more extreme this delusion can get. Without knowing it we can end up feeding a fantasy instead of sincerely looking within.

Investing in such fictitious ideas is what being ungrounded is all about. The ego wants to feel strengthened and it wants to be entertained. By using grand concepts, it manages to create a mental world which it can enjoy. When the current situation is not spicy enough, when it all appears mundane, the ego looks for something extraordinary, something that will captivate us. It re-interprets our circumstances in a way which gives us the enjoyment we have been craving. Ideas are manufactured to deal with the unfulfillment we feel on our path.

One of the key symptoms of being ungrounded is incessant speculation. When we do not want to engage with the reality in front of us, we love to constantly wonder and ask questions about things we may never know the answer to, or we enjoy making up reasons for why things are happening. Our minds dwell on things which have no real relevance to our path. The ego wants to make us discuss and create explanations that we cannot prove. Rather than have a strict focus on spiritually growing, it does whatever it can to escape it.

If we sit back and let this happen, we can drift away into delusional worlds. Our feelings get whipped up and we start believing in things which have no basis. We no longer remain an innocent spiritual seeker who is just starting out, we can end up believing we are a unique soul with a profound purpose. Of course, there is truth in this. Each of us is different and has indeed been born to specifically attain something. But the ego manipulates this concept and uses it to elevate us above everyone else. We slip into a mindset where we are convinced, we are special, even chosen. The ego wants to feel empowered and it does this by making us congratulate ourselves on spiritual achievements that have not been achieved. It fools us by confusing fantasies with genuine experience. This is easily done, and it is one of the greatest dangers on the spiritual path. Because there is no obvious way of certifying inner states, one can easily pretend to have them. If there is no evidence to prove or disprove our experience, we can justify almost anything to ourselves.

Sometimes, the fantasies are outlandish, and involve experiencing energies and spiritual powers. Most of the time they are more subtle. Things like the humble austere saint who incessantly sacrifices himself, the knowledgeable teacher who delivers wisdom, the great devotee who steps out and preaches to the world, or the pure soul who cries longingly for God, can all seem like examples worthy of emulation. Theoretically they embody all that we are striving to achieve. It seems perfectly reasonable to do what we can to follow their example. The problem is we can emulate them in the wrong way. When we overly romanticise the external appearance, with no clue about the internal state, we can think we know who they are, but all we are really doing is projecting our understanding onto them. There is no appreciation of what is required to manifest these ideals. We do not recognise the level of detachment, the amount of humility and intensity that is required.

Instead of trying to genuinely achieve these examples of spiritual advancement, we try to imitate them. We change our habits and character to copy what we hold in our mind. The way we carry ourselves, the way we talk, our outlook on life all attempt to replicate our projected idea of holiness.

The image of being intense and driven is enticing. We think that when we shed tears, meditate or make some sacrifice we are living out the qualities of saints and yogis, but none of it is really based on inner transformation. Being ungrounded is all about denying who we truly are for the glamour of what we want or think we ought to be. It is where we neglect the truth within, and we run after the ego's projection.

The Ego Confuses Beliefs with Convictions and Realisation

The problem of being ungrounded arises when we confuse belief, conviction and realisation. For example, when we are told that we are the soul, if we understand it on a purely mental level, then this is a belief. If deep inside ourselves we feel that our true identity cannot be material and must be transcendent, then we have more than a belief, we have a conviction. If we have the full experience of being a soul, beyond any thought, or even any feeling, we have realisation.

Beliefs are ideas that we use to navigate our path. We need something for the mind to hold onto, a narrative, a theoretical system that identifies a goal and allows us to move towards it. Almost every religion, tradition or spiritual movement has a narrative that gives us an understanding of why and where we are going. Convictions are more than beliefs; they are truths that we feel in our heart. They are based on an inner revelation that we trust. The feeling that our life has a purpose and the recognition that it is being guided is an example of this. Realisation however, is much more. It is what has directly become known in our experience. It is not a narrative or an understanding, nor is it something we strongly feel. Realisation is what we have seen directly. Like our very existence, there is no doubting it.

The ego often tries to convince us that our superficial

beliefs are convictions or even realisations. The ego takes ideas that we do not really understand and makes us believe we have fully internalised them. Instead of directly experiencing them, we mentally make up the experience. The ego enjoys fooling us into believing we are advancing, because that way we remain significant, successful and legitimate.

But the true test of where we stand is revealed when life challenges us. Realisations are totally untouched by any external circumstances; they are beyond this material experience. If we trust our convictions, they provide an anchor that keeps us focused and helps us weather the storm. Beliefs however quickly disintegrate in the face of difficulties because there is no foundation behind them. There is no internal support for these ideas. One minute we might declare that God is the controller of everything, the next we claim that He does not even exist. A path built solely on beliefs is weak and unsteady. In any moment the ego can make us throw them to one side for another set of ideas that serves us better.

There is a vicious cycle which keeps us ungrounded. The pursuit of pleasure prevents us from going deep and experiencing the divine presence within, and consequently we end up feeling the spiritual path is not satisfying enough. Because we become bored, we look to fantasies that arouse our interest. The more we feed them, the less deep we can go, so the more we seek superficial pleasure. On and on it goes until somehow, a life situation shocks us out of it. Ungrounded tendencies are weeds which can turn into forests. We can carry them in some form or another for years, thinking they are based in truth. They are however, another tactic the ego uses to deceive us.

Duryodhana Manipulates Karna and Dhritarashtra – The Ego Uses Relationships for Its Own End

Duryodhana is a centrifugal force that draws vulnerable individuals under his control. He seizes upon Dhritarashtra and Karna in particular. One of them clears the way for his plans to unfold, the other is manipulated for his military skill. Ultimately, they are not people, but pawns to be used.

The ego plays the same role in our relationships. It relentlessly tries to calculate how much value the other person has, and how best to exploit it. In our lives it is rare to find relationships which are entirely run by the ego, but at the same time, it is extremely rare to find ones where the ego is completely absent. While we might sincerely care about the friends and family around us, in some way we are likely to be using them. Relationships are complex with many intentions and emotions woven together. No one likes to admit that the bonds with family friends are anything but noble and pure. Even though we may genuinely feel love and loyalty for another person, it is quite possible that amongst these sentiments, there is an intention to use them. Along with our selfless feelings, the ego part of us is out to get what it wants. Even whilst caring for someone we can still expect them to be a certain way that suits us.

If we unconsciously allow the ego to take charge, we end up choosing relationships in a specific way. We need people who will provide support and legitimacy to our behaviour. Ideally, friends should not have strong opinions because if they do, then there is a chance they will tell us truths that expose our real intentions. Just like Duryodhana is surrounded by elders such as Vidura who are willing to expose his falsehood, there are potentially people around us who could unveil the ego's deceitful tactics. Therefore, the ego is careful to stay clear of them, or at least keep them at a distance. Instinctively it knows who is on its side and who is not.

The ego can also use relationships to hide the problems we have inside. Just as spiritual activities can be a distraction, so can people. When we have friends, who are willing to entertain us, we don't have to contend with the issues within. The aim is to be as busy as possible. This means creating a jam-packed schedule filled with events. We need a hectic social life, something that will fill the time and make us forget our problems.

Over time the ego can form groups of people who act like a support network. They provide a feeling that everything is alright. On the surface it looks like we have a cosy group of friends who we genuinely like, and to a large extent that is the case. We care about their lives, we share stories and enjoy good humour. But beneath this are a series of connections which feed the ego's agenda. We may not know it, but the ego is using these friendships to cover up the things we should be looking at.

Ego-Based Relationships Vs Spiritual Relationships

Duryodhana constantly has Karna, Shakuni, and Dushasana by his side, because they are loyal to his cause. They have made a commitment to give their lives to him.

The ego too wants this level of commitment from others. This is what makes us needy and desperate. There is an urgent requirement to keep others under our control. Either we have a certain image we want to maintain, or more commonly we are insecure and need people to support us. As soon as our 'friends' start breaking the mould and deviating from their role, things begin to crumble. When they are no longer willing to hear our depressing story, or feed our opinions, we feel like our trust has been betrayed. When instead of supporting all that we do, they begin to unleash uncomfortable truths, it seems like we have been stabbed in the back. The ego is never interested in self-reflection; everything is the fault of others. Even if everybody around is telling us that we are wrong, our reflex is to always assume they are the ones who have changed for the worse and abused our trust.

Ego based relationships are on a knife edge because they are founded on pure expectation. Ultimately these friendships are business deals designed to give us what we want. As we enter into them, our unconscious mind draws up a contract with terms and conditions. We sign on the dotted line, and we assume the other party has as well. Like all businesses there is a balance sheet where profits have to outweigh losses. The benefits must be worth the sacrifices. As long as we act from the ego, we have yet to fully appreciate what makes a relationship unconditional.

Unconditional means seeing a higher purpose for the other person, and willingly helping that person grow towards that. In other words, the relationship should have a goal, which both individuals are willing to strive for. This is the difference between spiritual and ego-based relationships. Whereas the ego is all about indulging the other, spiritual relationships are founded on service. Each person willingly puts in the time and effort to help the other change and evolve. In its purest form, there are no expectations and no demands.

If we do not strive for this higher ideal, our relationships will simply be a series of exchanges between two egos. Far from helping the other to rise to a higher goal, we will actively try and stop them. There is the constant fear that we will be abandoned. The other person's spiritual development is a threat because it signals the end of the contract. The ego can no longer own them.

As we develop spiritually, restrictive relationships are naturally severed. Inevitably, those who are moving forward on their path vibrate at a different level. This vibration attracts certain people and also repels others. If we are ego driven, we will suddenly feel we do not know the other person. There is a breakdown in the connection. Before we felt close and at home, now we feel miles apart. As this happens, the ego slowly sees our friend becoming an enemy. Nothing has changed on the outside, but it becomes clear that we are losing them.

Depending on how unconscious we are, the ego is willing to use whatever means necessary to keep the other person under our control. We blame them by saying how they have changed. We complain that they have become selfish and ungrateful for everything we have done for them, or even that they are neglecting their responsibility to us. In whatever way possible, the ego will try to get them to stick to the terms of the contract.

Duryodhana has no anxiety at the prospect of destroying his whole family and bringing suffering to millions. He wants the kingdom and will not yield even an inch of it to save bloodshed. In the same way the ego does not care about the consequences. It wants what it wants. Either by tyrannical oppression or through emotional blackmail, the ego will try to make others bend to its wishes.

Duryodhana Meets Krishna – The Ego Cannot Recognise the Master

After abusing the Pandavas and sending them to exile, Duryodhana refuses to give back their share of the kingdom. Now that war is a certainty, he marches to Dwarka to see Krishna. Duryodhana is all too aware that He holds the key to victory. There is no one who can match His power and knowledge. Whoever has Krishna on their side is guaranteed to win the kingdom. With this in mind, Duryodhana shamelessly poses as a dear friend. Pointing out their family ties, he pretends he has some kind of right to ask for Krishna's support in the war. Unfortunately for him Arjuna too arrives. When given the choice, Arjuna rejects the powerful army of the Yadavas and chooses an unarmed Krishna who has vowed not to fight. Duryodhana is both baffled and overjoyed at this decision. He gleefully laughs at what he sees as Arjuna's foolish naivety.

Krishna is the Supreme Truth we are all looking to attain. In the face of this Truth, we see the sharp distinction between someone who is driven by the ego and someone who is moved by a heart that is yearning to grow spiritually. In reality, both situations exist within us and influence our behaviour at different times. Sometimes we seek to aggressively make demands on life, other times we are grateful and accepting. The dynamic between the ego and the heart becomes especially apparent when Divinity takes the form of the spiritual Master.

The ego makes us blind. Like Duryodhana, it cannot recognise the Master. When He appears in our life as a Person, the reality of who He is and the opportunity He presents cannot be appreciated. No matter how much the ego tries to work Him out, it always hits a brick wall. It does not have the tools to digest the immensity of what He is. It can only understand the physical circumstances around Him: What crowds does he gather? How many centres does He have? Are His words pleasing and favourable? The ego uses superficial features to measure the infinite nature of Divinity.

Arjuna however, is a devotee and bows with humility at Krishna's feet. He is not here to do business but to meet God. Similarly, it is this sincerity that allows us to see the truth of the Master. We cut through the external persona and perceive His divinity. A devotee trusts the wisdom of their heart over the chaos of the mind. There is no judgement or calculation of what the Master does, only a deep reverence for the Divinity He embodies. Just as Duryodhana cannot understand Arjuna, the ego cannot comprehend devotion. It sees it as illogical and foolish. Often a devotee is mistakenly viewed as a simpleton, somebody who is gullible and overly sentimental. The ego does not understand the secret in their hearts, the secret which allows them to see God.

Arjuna's decision is crystal clear. Even though the army is one of the largest, most powerful groups of soldiers, there is simply no comparison with God Himself; it all means nothing without Krishna. If we are a true devotee, what matters is who the Master is, not what the Master has. His achievements, His charisma, even His miraculous nature are all beautiful ornaments, but they do not define our faith. The relationship exists at a completely different level. It is soul to soul and does not depend on externals. Arjuna has this wisdom. He can see through the veil of the Master because he has a heart which is truly longing for God.

It is this longing that qualifies us to grasp Him as He really is. Whereas the ego pushes us towards judgement, humility opens the door to insight; the two exist in different realities. Just as Arjuna knows Krishna is infinitely more than His army, a true devotee understands that the Master is infinitely more than what our mind understands. Nothing outside of Him is worth pursuing. Duryodhana has no such yearning, which is why Arjuna's choice leaves him utterly baffled.

Duryodhana Takes the Army – The Ego Uses the Master

Almost everyone who goes to the Master is always seeking something. A sincere devotee is using Him to satisfy his yearning for the Divine. They are clear they are going to the ultimate person to find the ultimate solution. When our relationship is defined by the ego, the dynamic is completely different. So long as the Master plays the game to our expectations, we are loyal to Him. When He conforms to our ideas, we follow like a lovesick puppy. We become a dedicated disciple, diligently serving at every turn. At all times we are eager to promote and protect Him.

It looks like sincerity, but in reality, it is another way in which we have become ungrounded. Instead of being a real devotee, the ego makes us more like a pop star groupie. Our emotions are over the top and we are easily excitable. The Master is like a drug that we use for cheap highs. Because we are so dedicated externally, we confuse our fanatic behaviour with love. We believe that obsessively running after Him is somehow a reflection of how much our heart is longing. We approach the Master not to patiently receive, but to grab for gratification. There is little interest in surrendering and almost no motivation to look within. Duryodhana only wants an army to give him victory, he has no need for Krishna Himself. In the same way as long as the Master keeps delivering on the outside, the ego is engaged. There is little interest in who He truly is.

This kind of behaviour is not limited to the Master Himself. If we cannot access Him directly, we can often find ourselves acting out the same thing with those who have proximity to Him. Individuals who have a 'higher' profile and display various talents become superstar personalities worthy of our worship. Because we do not have the strength and focus to win the grace of the Master directly, we settle for lesser alternatives. The ego treats these people as if they were gurus simply because of their personality and charisma. We do not dote on them because we want to develop or follow their example, but because it is easier and they are more accessible. Instead of using them for inspiration, the ego uses them as cheap alternatives to the Master Himself.

When we offer praise sincerely, it is done from a place of gratitude. It is a natural outpouring after seeing how much the Master has changed our lives. When we recognise His glory, we become eager to declare it to the world. The ego also praises the Master, but from a completely different place. Duryodhana does not hold back when declaring his friendship to Krishna and is quick to exaggerate how strong their relationship is. So too whenever the ego encounters the Master, it is desperate to be noticed. Externally we can behave like a humble servant, but internally we cannot stop running after His recognition.

We think that through flattery, we can win Him over. Like an empty drum, we get carried away, overly glorifying how great He is. We recklessly shout out our undying love for Him without actually meaning it. When we are not sincere, the loudness of our praise becomes a reflection of how superficial we are. Genuine devotion comes from a longing heart, this is what makes us glorify Him as much as possible. But when the ego dictates what we say, there is only hot air and hype. In place of authentic prayers that spring forth from within, we shout out praises to gain attention.

Rather than pleasing the Master, the ego tries to make us impress Him. Pleasing means we see the Master's Divinity. We understand that He is life itself and so we honour Him by doing our duty. We realise that fulfilling the purpose we have been born for is the best way to make Him happy.

Impressing the Master is where our ego makes us treat Him as an ordinary person. We think that by displaying our talent and accomplishing big projects we can gain His approval. We want Him to applaud and marvel at how well we are doing. To get His attention we do things like boldly announce how much we love Him or how everything we have belongs to Him. We do not realise the gravity of the statements we are making. Delivering grand devotional declarations is enjoyable. At a deeper level, the ego wants to control Him. Just like Duryodhana seeks to manipulate Krishna through his gestures and words, it too tries to draw the Master into its game. Regardless of what genuine connection we have with Him, we want to be praised and honoured as one of His closest and most distinguished devotees.

Duryodhana Tries to Take Krishna Prisoner – How the Ego Attempts to Capture the Master

When Krishna comes as a peace ambassador, He urges Duryodhana to see sense. He explains that this impending war is not inevitable, but His words fall on deaf ears and Duryodhana refuses to yield. Enraged at Krishna's words he seeks to bind and take Him prisoner.

When the Master tries to rescue us and make us change, His instructions are like arrows that cut deep. We cannot listen to them. Instead of reflecting on the wisdom, we become deeply offended.

If the Master no longer reflects the way we see life, His compassion is received as poison. We lose trust in Him and question His motives. We begin to wonder what He wants from us. Only a moment ago we were openly declaring how we were ready to sacrifice our life for His mission. Now that He is no longer playing the game we want, everything abruptly changes. The doubts start creeping in and we become suspicious. The ego starts proposing different ideas. Is He just using us for His own ends? Maybe He wants us for our talents and wealth? In a short space of time the relationship which was supposed to be the centre of our life deteriorates. Arrogance brings ingratitude. Suddenly all that the Master has done for us, all the sacrifices and blissful moments He gave us are overlooked. The ego transforms somebody who was once our saviour into an enemy.

Duryodhana sees Krishna as an obstacle to success, an outsider who has no business meddling with his plan. Angered at His incessant attempts to strip him of his kingdom, he tries to take Krishna prisoner. Now we see the Master as a barrier, somebody who has been holding us back. The absurdity is that He has been the only person who has truly had our interests at heart. But because He is no longer meeting our demands, the ego creates a radically warped perspective. It will not allow us to admit that our loss of trust has happened due to our failed expectations. We have not received the attention and privileges we once had, so we have turned our back on Him. The ego made a deal, a contract that the Master was supposed to stick to and He has strayed from the agreement without our consent.

These toxic thoughts arise because we do not understand that the Master is here to free our soul, not to grant our desires. In the beginning He will do what is needed to initiate the thirst for Truth. Seeing the potential that is there, He does the necessary to awaken it. There comes a point where the ego stops the flowering of this potential, and this is where it needs to be challenged head on. If we are stubborn, if we refuse to change, then direct intervention is needed. It means the Master telling us things we do not wish to hear and identifying issues that we want to ignore. Out of love, He confronts the ego and urges us to change course.

Eventually, just like Duryodhana the ego attempts to bind and bring Him under control. It does this by projecting a negative false version of Him. Even though we are still devotees on the outside, internally we start to turn against Him. We start creating stories about how He no longer cares about us. We begin to judge and find faults in His actions. The ego distorts reality and suddenly all that is good about the Master is stripped away. It knows if His message is accepted, if His words are taken as wisdom, then automatically we will have to admit we are wrong, and we will have to rethink our whole life. Therefore the ego has to put His Divinity to one side and treat Him as a human.

Like Krishna, the Master's Divinity cannot be contained by the mind. God cannot be locked up in anyone's narrative or expectation. Every time we try to bind the Master, He breaks free. Every box we put Him in, is broken out of, every framework is dismantled, every judgement is made redundant. When Duryodhana gives the order to capture Him, Krishna reveals His cosmic form. All those present behold the elements of creation and the celestial deities within His body. The entire assembly is forced into awe and humble submission. Shockingly, in spite of this revelation, Duryodhana cannot be convinced. He writes off the whole affair as some conjuring trick. Humiliated and frustrated at his failure, he storms out of the courtroom.

The ego has an amazing resilience. Even when confronted with God, even when it comes face to face with Truth it still manages to work out a justification for not changing. Internally, if we want to reject the Master, there is a problem: We have seen in our life how the Master orchestrates events. We have witnessed how He has always selflessly cared and served our best interest. What do we do with all the grace we have been given?

To get around this, the many lessons that built our relationship have to be reinterpreted. The ego has to create a new script that fits the story we have made. In whatever way possible, we play down the extraordinary experiences we received. We ignore all the help that was given. The innumerable blessings and the unconditional Love we have been shown have to be dismissed. This is not easy to do. It means suppressing feelings and burying insights we know to be true. If we fail to do this, once again we will be forced to backtrack and accept that the Master is right and we are wrong.

The ego of Duryodhana shows how a shallow attitude prevents us from fulfilling our potential. The relentless hunt for pleasure, the search for power and control are what take us away from our path. If we want to follow the Master, we need to access a different space inside ourselves. We need to escape the rat race of running after quick, superficial experiences. The true nature of Divinity cannot be sampled on a surface level, It has to be dived into. The spiritual path only works if we are ready to commit ourselves long term and give everything we have. We need to develop an uncompromising, firm resolve that we stick to at all costs. Only then can Duryodhana be defeated.

Life Lessons Rising Beyond the Hypocrisy of Duryodhana

- **Work Out When the Ego is Using the Spiritual Path**

  It is important that we understand the difference between having a spiritual lifestyle and walking a spiritual path. Spirituality is a broad term that includes a range of ideas and practices. These can be useful to de-stress, to control the mind and to provide focus and meaning. A spiritual path, however, is very specific: It means having a clear goal, and a clear intention to transform. It means we are seeking to override our lower selfish desires for something higher. It is crucial we know where we stand between the two. The reason why we use and abuse, why we jump from one thing to another, is because we have no real purpose. Before doing anything, we need to take a breath, to pause and seriously question what we want.

  Is realising who we are our aim? Do we even know what that means? Our minds can learn all kinds of rehearsed, plausible answers, but these profound questions have to be answered more by what we feel within, then by simply what we think.

Even though there may be a part of us that is yearning to grow spiritually, we cannot pretend that is all we are. There are other parts of ourselves that want other things. Having a goal does not mean we have to have perfect exclusive devotion. It does mean we should always try to answer our higher calling above the other options available. We may not achieve it every time, but at least we understand what we should be working towards. The more we put the Divine first, the more the other parts of who we are start to wither away. As this happens, we grow in sincerity.

<u>Practical Step</u>: Perform a series of thought experiments and see what you would readily give up for your spiritual path and what you would struggle to let go of. Think of your relationships, your possessions and your lifestyle. How easy would it be to renounce them?

Very few people are ready to renounce everything, nor does the spiritual path demand that we do such a thing. It does, however, require us to be internally detached. Asking these kinds of questions, gives some indication of where we stand. The level of detachment from the world provides an idea of how committed we are to this path and how much we want to change.

- **Develop the Quality of Servitude**

  Instead of always having things on our terms, there has to be a willingness to take on a degree of austerity. Carrying out our spiritual duties is a wonderful thing, but when our service fits what we like, we can easily make it more about ourselves, and forget that we are here to serve others. How sincere we are is all about how much we are able to put ourselves to one side, and work for a higher cause. Ideally, our enthusiasm should not be from the act we are doing, but rather from the satisfaction of dedicating everything to our higher purpose.

  This state takes time to develop. The more we can override the ego's pull towards pleasure, the more we can develop within. As this happens, fulfilling our higher purpose becomes more attractive than satisfying the ego. The task of moving past selfish, shallow desires gets easier and less arduous. We realise that what we want is limited and what life wants for us is unlimited. Little by little, our spiritual practice and activities start to take on a different quality. We move past the childish immaturity that makes everything about us. Eventually the heart to heart connection with the Divine becomes more important than any praise or success. Then we see that the best things are performed out of the limelight, where nobody but us knows what has been done.

Practical Step: Every week do some kind of service which does not immediately pander to what you like. If possible, make sure nobody knows you are doing it and silently offer the task to the Divine.

- **Know that the Ego Makes Us Ungrounded:**

To deal with being ungrounded we need to have little or no expectation from our spiritual path. There can be a temptation to constantly try and work out how much progress we are making. The strong need for some kind of validation can compel us to run after dramatic experiences and when we do not see what we are looking for, it can be tempting to make it up. The best attitude is to practice and serve without any interest in what results might come up. Expectation itself is a barrier to growth. Rather than constantly waiting for some big experience, we need to cultivate an attitude of seeing everything we do as an offering to our higher purpose. Any transformation our practice brings will happen at the right time if we are sincere.

Practical Step: Accept the possibility that whatever spiritual techniques you are doing are going to be done for the rest of your life without any reward or experience. In that spirit, learn to enjoy the practice itself and not the expected fruit of it.

To really get to grips with being ungrounded, it is critical to adopt an attitude which is ruthlessly based on facts. That means we have to be comfortable confessing what we do not know. Being ungrounded is all about carelessly straying away from what is true and using ideas we know nothing about. To deal with this, we have to ask ourselves what we know for sure. What knowledge do we have that is utterly indisputable? We know for instance, that we exist, and we know that death will come at some point. If we are really honest, there are not many more things we can add to this.

To be grounded we must be cautious about ideas and how much we invest in them. As much as possible we should strive to repeatedly come back to the raw foundations of what we are certain about. Being grounded is to constantly live by what we really know, not on what we wish to be true. We have to throw away the subtle enjoyment we derive from speculative thinking.

Having said this, there are certain things we do take on faith. For example everything that happens, is happening for a reason. This faith begins with a mental belief, develops into an inner conviction and concludes into full realisation. We must discern which level we are at. Insincerity is when we have a mental belief and act like it is a conviction or even an absolute realisation. It is where we get carried away and pretend we know things we do not.

Practical Step: With every spiritual idea you think and talk about, ask yourself how relevant it is to reaching your goal. If it is relevant, then analyse at what level you know it. How much has come from ideas you have learned from others, and how much is what you independently feel in your heart regardless of what everybody else thinks?

- **Understand How the Ego Works In Relationships:**

Sincerity to our spiritual goal also means being sincere to the people around us. The way we are with others is a reflection of our devotion. While all relationships are important, there is a greater responsibility with those who are on the same path. A spiritual community carries a flow of grace, and it is important that everyone who is part of it looks to honour that grace. We do this by constantly helping one another to grow.

At the same time, it is important to realise that we are all at various levels of spiritual evolution, so naturally relationships will also be at different levels. The ideal of serving and pushing each other to the Divine is something that will gradually become more intense as we advance. Eventually, as we grow, it will be the only thing that sustains all our relationships.

<u>Practical Step</u>: With every friend or relative, identify a source of meaning that is higher than what you personally want from them and what they might want from you. Then try to make the purpose of your relationship about both of you reaching that goal.

- **Beware of Using the Master**

In the initial stages of the spiritual path, it is normal to use the Master for attention and enjoyment. When the foundation of our relationship is weak, we must take opportunities to build that connection. A child needs encouragement and praise to cement their confidence, but as it matures that need diminishes. So too there comes a point when the constant hankering for approval and affirmation has to fall away. The spark of joy that was so important at the beginning, should develop into something deeper. As we follow the Master, it should dawn on us that our relationship means so much more than passing moments of validation.

We have to end this contractual business relationship and cultivate something deeper. Our bond with the Master is eternal and not merely dependent on what we are being given on the outside. When we understand this, it slowly becomes clear that the goal of our spiritual path is not happiness. It is not about satisfying desires; it is about finding a transcendent state beyond this world. When we realise this, we will not run to Him to be boosted or recognised. We do not want passing highs. Whenever we are in His presence, rather than be shallow and superficial we will have a sense of responsibility and there will be a deep yearning to realise who He truly is.

<u>Practical Step</u>: Expand your vision of the Master and know He is present in all situations. Remember that external achievements and praise do not please Him, honouring your path and inner transformation does.

Dhritarashtra – The Hypocrisy of Refusing Responsibility

Dhritarashtra sat stunned listening to his charioteer. Through the grace of Vyasa, Sanjaya had been given the vision to see everything on the battlefield. The blind king had been sitting on his throne hearing the events as they unfolded. Before the conches were blown, he had immense confidence that his son would emerge victorious. Bhishma was in command. He was unconquerable and could choose the time of his death. Drona was next in line and had taught the Pandavas all they knew. Then there was Karna, perhaps the only warrior who could match the prowess of Arjuna. The Kauravas had everything in their favour. Added to this, Duryodhana's armies significantly outnumbered Yudhishthira's. It was only a matter of time before the kingdom would be celebrating the coronation of his beloved son.

Now the blind king was in a daze. During the last few  minutes, he had heard from Sanjaya about the stunning conversation between Krishna and Arjuna on the battlefield. He was overwhelmed by the wisdom that had transpired, but more than that he was terrified by the description of the cosmic form. Krishna was clear – He had already slaughtered the enemies of the Pandavas. Fate had been decided. He listened to how all the great warriors had been helplessly devoured by the gnashing teeth of destiny. He did not know how to digest the scene, but Sanjaya's cutting words made it clear 'Wherever there is Krishna, and wherever there is Arjuna there will surely be victory'. It was the last nail in the coffin. The blind king knew it – Duryodhana was as good as dead.

He began asking himself how had it come to this? Could he have done something? Could he have stopped this calamity? He broke down as he saw how stupid these questions were.

Dhritarashtra was the king, he had sovereign rule, he had the last say in all matters. If anyone could have prevented this disaster, it was him.

He remembered that when Duryodhana was born, the whole kingdom was flooded with evil omens. He was told that his child was a demon who would bring destruction to the Kuru clan. Vidura and others insisted that he be discarded there and then. Either he was eliminated, or the kingdom would face ruin. The signs were clear and Dhritarashtra knew they were right, but his toxic attachment had already begun.

Years later when Duryodhana invited the Pandavas to Varnavat, he ordered them to go knowing full well his son was planning to burn them alive. When the kingdom was divided in half, he deliberately gave his son Hastinapura, and to Yudhishthira the dry barren land of Khandavaprastha. Dhritarashtra watched as the Pandavas transformed it into the most opulent city on Earth. When Duryodhana's jealousy reached boiling point, he buckled and agreed to Shakuni's gambling match. Despite being aware that the Pandavas would be cheated, he invited them anyway. This was the point of no return.

While sitting on his throne he watched as they were stripped of their kingdom and their dignity. He sat silent as Draupadi was disgraced and hounded by his sons. Her miraculous vindication was a rude awakening that struck fear in his heart. God was not on Duryodhana's side. The king had to act fast to fix this horrific situation. At Draupadi's request, he gave back all that was lost. But yet again, the wailing of his son forced him to change his mind. He ignored the catastrophe that had just happened and called the Pandavas back for a second game. As expected Shakuni worked his magic and had them banished to the forest.

After their exile, he remembered urging Yudhishthira to reconsider war. Dhritarashtra was shameless. Despite all the suffering the Pandavas had endured at the hands of his son, he insisted they just submit and accept Duryodhana's decision. As a last effort for peace, Krishna came to the palace urging his son to finally see sense. He recalled the shocking vision where he saw the cosmic form of the Lord. This was the first and last time his eyes had been opened. In those few moments he had seen everything that needed to be seen. Krishna was God, the Lord of all. But somehow even this direct revelation was not enough to move him.

Dhritarashtra knew what dharma was. He always understood the responsibility he had as king. Vidura, his minister, was the wisest man in the kingdom. He never stopped shining a light on his cowardice. He incessantly warned him against his decisions, but the king never heeded his counsel. Duryodhana's hold was too strong. At every turn he refused to take action. He remembered that day Vidura left the palace. Furious at the insults of Duryodhana, he abandoned his position and stormed out. Dhritarashtra's heart was broken, he knew in that moment dharma had finally left him.

Despite having all the power, in the face of every calamity

he always pleaded helplessness: What could he do against the will of his son? "We are all victims of fate," he repeatedly told himself. Such a deceitful philosophy masked his ulterior motives. The truth was, he never wanted righteousness, only the glory of Duryodhana. His neglect and indulgence meant he would have to stomach the slaughter of all his children. This whole tragedy was entirely his doing.

Dhritarashtra Pretends to Follow Dharma While Protecting Duryodhana – When We Pretend to Do Our Duty Whilst Serving the Ego[3]

Perhaps the one character in the Mahabharata who could have ended the tyranny of Duryodhana, was Dhritarashtra. Every other person had an opinion and some influence, but Dhritarashtra was the king, and if he had just willed it, justice would have prevailed. Had he taken a stand against his son at any point, his family would have been saved.

Through his actions we are made aware of the disastrous consequences of neglect. We often think that it is only by actively doing things that mistakes are made, but a lack of action over time is equally destructive. Life is on the move, and the spiritual path requires us to keep up and change. What was good now may not be good

[3] Paramahamsa Vishwananda, Bhagavad Gita, page 32.

enough tomorrow, what worked before may no longer be appropriate. We have to be vigilant, sensitive and above all responsible. If we stand still, opportunities will move away from us. The gap between where we are and where we should be will increase. Overlooking our responsibility, is what leads to spiritual stagnation and provides the optimum conditions for the ego's growth.

Duryodhana's birth stands for the ego's initial appearance. This can be triggered in any number of ways, but when it first emerges there are sinister signs: We might feel excessively satisfied if we do something right, or we could have a sense of guilt as we enjoy being praised. If we honestly analyse ourselves, we can recognise when our pride is starting to take hold.

The wise thing to do is cut down the ego in its infancy. We have to immediately stop giving energy to it, by redirecting our thoughts and remembering what our path is really about. Instead of revelling in success, we need to bow down to all the things that have helped us. In whatever way possible our thoughts need to be trained to come back to a place of humility. The longer we leave it, the more attachment we build to the ego's presence. Eventually we can lose the ability to detect it and then we risk it controlling us. Because Dhritarashtra refuses to slay Duryodhana at birth, instead of ruling a kingdom, he is ruled by his son. So too inaction allows the ego to grow into a dictator that dominates our whole spiritual path.

Dhritarashtra is a man who is torn. While condemning Duryodhana's actions before the elders, he simultaneously claims he is helpless to stop him. He pleads with Duryodhana to see sense, but at the same time clears the way for him to carry out his plans. Dhritarashtra knows what righteousness is, but he also wants the ambition of his son to be fulfilled. The result is a duplicitous, devious king. His noble words conceal and buy time for Duryodhana to get what he wants. In front of Vidura and Bhishma he is the righteous ruler of Hastinapura, but behind closed doors, he is complicit in conspiring to take down the Pandavas. Dhritarashtra is on a tightrope constantly trying to survive the opinions of others, whilst supporting his son. His unwillingness to control Duryodhana invokes the suspicion of those around him. He knows the pressure is on and the judgement of his actions is mounting.

When we build an attachment to the ego, we too are standing in two boats. On one hand we can see what we should be doing, we understand the right course of action, but at the same time we are being pulled to fulfil the ego's needs. If we remain in this limbo place without taking a stand then nothing we do is clean and straightforward. We end up being complicated individuals who have to play complicated games. Like Dhritarashtra, we dodge and make excuses to get our way. We make up whatever stories are needed to cover our tracks and hide our true intentions. Whilst trying to conform to people's expectations, we do the best we can to satisfy the ego's needs.

To stop others analysing our faults, we can often talk about how important it is not to judge others. Whenever there are people who do not seem to be hitting the mark, we try and stand up for them as much as possible. It seems like we are being loyal and kind, but really, we are worried that the judgement levelled at them will eventually fall on us. The whole task of the ego is to avoid being exposed. It has to be tactical. There will be some situations where we have to give in and do what is right, but other times where possible we can escape and have our way.

Responsibility means being accountable, it means we cannot act as we please. In contrast the ego wants pleasure and that means doing what we like when we like. It cannot tolerate people pointing the finger at us, nor does it want questions being asked, or results expected. The ego is after a world on its terms, one where we do not have to answer to anyone. Responsibility therefore endangers its whole plan. When we have to perform work which does not satisfy our desires, we are forced to be more selfless. Whenever we have to give up our time and resources, we naturally develop an attitude of servitude. The more this happens, the more the ego's pursuit of power cannot be sustained. Any form of commitment is a direct threat to its plans, which is why it is so keen to avoid it.

A sincere seeker goes as far as needed. They will take up whatever task is necessary for their path. They will not shy away from challenges. Rather than following their dreams they will follow their fears, confronting and moving past their inner demons. In contrast, when we align with the ego, we are careful to protect ourselves from being drawn in too deep. Consciously we want to believe we are serious spiritual seekers, so we put in a certain amount of effort. However, it is always the bare minimum, enough to satisfy our conscience, and anybody else who might point the finger, but not enough to encroach on our freedom. We do not dive in the water but only dip our toes in it.

Dhritarashtra's attachment to Duryodhana, stands for the weak resolve that the ego creates in us. Even when we know what is right, we do not have the strength or the courage to take decisive action. At the same time, we do not want the guilt of accepting our faults. In order to make this work, the ego becomes an expert at misusing self-analysis to validate our decisions. We tell ourselves that 'We must not become too rigid and dogmatic', or 'We must follow the spirit of the law not the letter.' The ego morphs rules into flexible guidelines which we can pick and choose, depending on our mood. The disciplines that were meant to protect our path end up becoming more elastic. 'It's OK' becomes a mantra that we use again and again. By developing a casual, carefree attitude, the ego gets the space it needs.

We often use these kinds of excuses to wriggle out of jobs we do not want to do. Sometimes we can pretend we are extremely busy, or that we have other duties which are far more important. Instead of taking the initiative for things, we always wait for a direct clear instruction which forces us to do it. When we do not like the role we have been given, the ego likes to tell us stories about how this cannot be what we have been born to do. We convince ourselves that the lack of enthusiasm we feel is a symptom of a higher purpose that is yet to happen. We do not want to accept that our work might be divinely ordained, that it might be an opportunity, perhaps a training for something greater. In the name of following a grander purpose we try to escape the tasks that have been given to us.

Dhritarashtra Fears the Death of Duryodhana – Protecting the Ego Makes Us Retreat from Life

Deep down Dhritarashtra knows that victory is on the Pandavas side. Even though he has a hundred sons, the five brothers cannot be defeated in open war. The strength of Bhima and the skill of Arjuna are too much for the Kauravas. As much as he can, Dhritarashtra tries to protect Duryodhana from death, but he does so in the most pathetic way. Even while on the brink of war, he gives Yudhishthira a lecture on dharma and pleads with him to simply give up and surrender. In the same way, if our priority is to protect the ego, not only is the spiritual path dangerous, but life itself is a threat.

Because life is random and chaotic; it has the potential to disturb everything. By its nature it calls for change, it wants us to come out, to experience and grow. There are opportunities to learn new things, to express our talents and form new relationships. Real living is all about stepping

110

out and exploring what lies beyond our comfort zone. The ego is afraid of this, and so tries to drag us back into our cave where it is safe. In an effort to shield ourselves from reality, we can end up becoming a recluse and retreat like a hermit. The ego wants security and predictability. It wants to maintain a place where obstacles do not come, and challenges do not disturb the peace. As much as possible it tries to kill our sense of adventure and have everything on its terms. Consequently, we are compelled to build a tailor-made house away from reality so that we can deal with life as it suits us.

The fear of what is 'out there' stops us achieving anything. We have no plans and no goals to aspire for. We live in the mind rejecting reality and pursuing fantasies. The more we do this, the more we end up becoming a dreamer. We enjoy living in mental worlds where all our desires can be played out. Imagining happiness is more appealing than actually going out and getting happiness. We find it satisfying to visualise perfect scenarios in our mind, but at the same time we rarely take any effort to make them come true. Even if these desires were to magically materialise, we would immediately reject them out of the fear of having to maintain them. Dreaming is far more appealing than reality; it provides what the ego is looking for: pleasure without responsibility. We can wonder and speculate without dealing with the consequences. There is no need to take action if we can be satisfied with illusions.

Self-isolation appears ascetic-like. It allows us to create

a belief that we are detached and above the world. In reality, we have become scared of life and we want to keep things the way we like them. This lack of participation is justified in a number of ways: Sometimes we can fool ourselves into believing we are doing 'inner work'. Instead of carrying out our duty, we say we are processing things within or doing important self-analysis. We tell people we need time to reflect on where we are going or that we need to focus more on our spiritual practice. The ego intentionally makes everything an internal process, so it can legitimise not doing anything externally. Instead of working and engaging, we can lie in bed thinking and wondering. We tell ourselves that we have to find 'God within', so there is no need to bother with any actual work. Everybody else is busying themselves with outside activities, because they do not have any longing and they have yet to discover an inner relationship. We do not see that real longing would automatically translate into action. It would naturally compel us to step out and engage in service. If we sincerely wanted to move forward, the last thing we would do is retreat from life and neglect our duty.

When our spiritual path is calling for us to be more intense in our commitment, another tactic the ego uses is to state how important it is to lead a 'balanced life'. Because we are unwilling to inwardly renounce the world, and are scared of the spiritual path, we declare how crucial it is to be 'normal'. We stress the importance of staying grounded and balanced. We talk about practicalities and fulfilling responsibilities. We avoid getting pulled into a path of renunciation by appearing pragmatic and well-reasoned. A similar thing happens when we become embarrassed about our path. If we are in an environment which does not readily accept what we believe, rather than standing strong and being honest about who we are, we become apologetic and cowardly. We find different ways to downplay how religious or spiritual we are. Instead of boldly owning our identity, we fear the judgement of others and try to protect our image.

The ego enjoys coming up with these stories, because they allow us to kick the can further down the road. We can tell ourselves how we should not force a change from what life has already laid out for us. Ironically, we talk about how we have to be sincere before committing to anything, not realising that the denial of our calling is itself a form of insincerity. 'One day' we tell ourselves, 'when God wills it, we will make the commitment'. We know that day will never come. But such statements provide comfort and make us feel we have not abandoned our purpose. The ego allows us to buy time and deflect any guilt we might feel. That way we can still believe we are doing the right thing, even if we are running away from our path.

The reason why the ego is on the run is that it knows engaging with life head on is engaging with Truth. This Truth will unravel the whole game it is playing with us. It will expose all its strategies. When we face responsibility, naturally the sacred potential within us will be drawn out.

The grace we carry will be brought to the surface. Following our duty initiates a churning process where we have to face fears, overcome insecurities and embrace transformation. The inevitable consequence is that the ego's plans will be destroyed. Responsibility directly invades and shakes our comfortable world. It causes the ego to come out and be dealt with directly. Dhritarashtra does everything possible to guard Duryodhana from this calamity. He tries to shield him from the scrutiny of the elders, and he pleads with Yudhishthira to abandon the war.

There is a limit to how long this can go on for. The more we are in denial, the more we feel the pressure of life. Constant inaction makes us repeatedly hit dead ends and realise we are going nowhere. Life repeatedly tries to show us that we cannot run from our dharma, we need to stand up and own our path.

Dhritarashtra's False Surrender – When Denial of Duty Masquerades as Acceptance of Divine Will

Whenever he is confronted, Dhritarashtra always pleads helplessness. He claims that each one of us is a victim of fate. We are innocent and have been manipulated by destiny. When life has decided on a certain course, who are we to take a stand? What can we possibly hope to achieve by fighting the tide? Such words sound noble and philosophical. To the innocent ear it seems like he has thought things through and given himself to the will of God. Dhritarashtra has managed to mask his refusal to act, as a form of devotional surrender. 'It is all God's will' is a much-abused term. When things follow the ego's expectations, we are led to believe in the power of fate and how everything happens for a reason. It is a useful idea to legitimise any situation we want.

Strangely whenever Duryodhana is troubled, Dhritarashtra is not so helpless. He manages to take decisive action, he sends the Pandavas to be potentially burnt alive, he unfairly gives them the barren land of Khandavaprastha, he even calls them back for a second game of dice. Dhritarashtra never fails to use his authority to carry out Duryodhana's bidding.

Similarly, when the ego's desires need to be met, we are made to quickly wake up. When there is something we want, or when our reputation is at stake, or even when there are rivals who may steal our glory, we are no longer content to leave things in the hands of the Divine. The ego cannot risk failure, so it forces us to step out to get what it wants. Now we are not so keen to talk about the 'will of God' or the 'nature of fate'. Suddenly we are somebody who makes their own destiny. We believe in action, and work. We are willing to fight and compete to make things happen. A switch has been flicked and we have a completely different philosophy. When we understand what is happening, the inconsistency in our behaviour makes sense: The truth is we have one master that is manipulating us – the ego; and both our inaction and action are satisfying its needs.

One ploy that looks like humility is to repeatedly state how unqualified we are. We can use this as a means to shy away from opportunities. Either we claim we do not have what it takes, or that there are other people better suited than us. This can easily get interpreted as a form of humility. The ego makes us play the timid, meek person, who stands at the back, retreating from fame and praise. If somehow, we are pulled into a situation against our will, we give a half-hearted effort and in extreme situations we can even find a subtle way of making it all fall apart. In reality what we want is to be left alone. Others might believe we are simple and innocent, above the glory of being in the limelight. But this passive attitude is just another persona the ego adopts to hide from the work we have to do.

Sometimes in the name of humility we can even start making ungrounded spiritual statements. We talk about how we do not have enough 'good karma' to be on a spiritual path. We lament at how fallen and undeserving we are. The grace of God is not with us, we say, and so maybe we are not meant to walk this path at all. Again, it appears as if we are innocent and submissive. Whenever we miss an opportunity to serve and grow, instead of admitting we did not take it, we use it as a sign that God has forsaken us. This is convenient, because if we can believe our higher calling has left us, we have a license to forsake it.

All these excuses simply hide the fact that we have given up on attaining any spiritual goal. We do not want to move on and evolve. Using so-called humble devotional narratives, we make progress seem impossible to attain, and that way we can be let off the hook from  even trying. The truth is we have lost enthusiasm, and we are not interested in changing. The world has given us enough, and the ego does not want the spiritual path to disturb the peace. We have fulfilled our desires, and it is time to relax.

If we are sincere in our intentions we do not hide behind such ideas. We know we are not always worthy; it is obvious we have innumerable faults, but this is no reason to write off our whole path. We trust that we can still move forward, and the presence of the Divine can guide us, so there is no question of retreating and running away. If anything, the acknowledgement of our flaws inspires us to work harder on ourselves. We want to do whatever we can to set things right. Any duty and opportunity is received with appreciation. If we truly want to transform, no amount of pseudo reasoning can stand in our way.

Instead of developing this strong resilience however, we develop exhaustion. The mind becomes tired. The constant requirement for introspection, the need to grow, the call for sacrifice, all take its toll. We wonder when we will finally gain peace. Sometimes we might claim we are even ready for death. We tell everyone that we are detached, and we want God so much that we are ready to leave the body at any moment. Such statements only reveal how much we have taken life for granted. God does not want us to die for Him, but to live for Him. In the name of devotion, we are keen to find a holy excuse to run away.

The thing we fail to understand is that the so-called peace we are hankering for has nothing to do with knowing our soul. Real peace lies in surrendering the mind and abandoning all desire, but we do not want to do that. The peace we crave is merely a cry for rest. The ego does not desire life, but sleep. We are not counting down the days until we meet God, but until we can do away with the responsibility of life.

While the ego brings fatigue, devotion makes us aware of the preciousness of life. Nothing is taken for granted. There is immense gratitude for the simple things. The people around us, the chance to serve even just to be alive are all looked upon as a gift. This mindset creates enthusiasm and drive. The ego wants to make us self-indulgent, but sincere gratitude gives us the energy to march forward and embrace change. Unlike Dhritarashtra, we understand that life is short, and we need to seize every chance.

Dhritarashtra Watches Duryodhana Disgrace the Pandavas – When Laziness and Neglect Give the Ego Full Control

Dhritarashtra can always justify to himself that he did

not directly have a hand in the war. Afterall he did not roll the dice that robbed the Pandavas of their wealth. This kind of logic allows Dhritarashtra to wash his hands of the situation. But even if this reasoning is true, it does not change the fact that he stood by and watched his nephews lose everything. When Draupadi was abused and disgraced, he did nothing to intervene. In the same way, our inaction eventually leads to the ego completely controlling us.

There are many factors that lead to this total dominance, such as fear or excessive attachment, but one of the most lethal is laziness. When things are appealing, we find immense enthusiasm. But when spiritual practice and work is needed, suddenly all our energy begins to dry up. We no longer have the drive; we do not want to push ourselves and unleash the potential we have inside. Everything becomes a chore and a burden. Laziness is the paralysis that sets in when there is nothing in it for the ego. It is where the ego captures and robs us of the ability to take action. This is not a small, innocent habit that can be ignored. It is a condition that runs the risk of ruining all spiritual progress.

We can all go through phases where our motivation is weak, but usually within a short space of time this passes. If we have really imbibed an attitude of service, then there is a natural energy that drives us. We can get up early in the morning when needed, we can work till late and we are ready to use up our free time for projects. Even if the

119

work is not particularly enjoyable, if it is needed, we are willing to take it on. While there is a limit to how hard anybody can push themselves, we are not afraid to graft to get the best results. In our hearts we know that we have been given a role and we want to do our best to honour it.

Laziness is where we have become so used to avoiding duty, so comfortable dodging what we have to do, that we automatically do it without thinking. There is no subconscious narrative dictating how we behave. The flaw has set into our body, so that on a physical level we cannot seize opportunities. Even when we know we are straying from the path, we are still unable to respond. In the gambling hall, Dhritarashtra witnesses the most abominable acts, but yet he sits unmoved. He does not have the will to intervene and stop Duryodhana. When we

are afflicted with laziness, we have become gagged and handcuffed by the ego. Even if we have the desire to change, even if we are ashamed of what we are doing, we do not have the energy to set things right.

Because of this lack of action, people and various opportunities around us can drift away. As this happens, it is easy to get drawn into our own personal world and believe that everything revolves around us. Laziness can make us increasingly self-indulgent. We only care about our opinions, what our circumstances are and what struggles we have to endure. When difficulties come, we act like we are the only people in the world who have ever had to face them. The ego causes us to have little or no appreciation for the efforts of others, or of how our behaviour is affecting them. Whenever we muster the strength to actually do some meaningful activity, we act like we have saved the world. We never stop talking about it, we are quick to advertise and claim credit for every little thing. Laziness makes us disproportionally over value our effort against everyone else.

Things can also go in the opposite direction. When we have nothing concrete to show for ourselves, we fail to create anything of value that justifies a purposeful existence. Day by day we see that we are wasting our life and so we start to doubt our self-worth. We lose confidence in who we are. Everybody else appears to be storming ahead while we are just getting older. Laziness eventually leads to a kind of self-loathing and makes us ashamed of what we have become. Even though Dhritarashtra does not stop Duryodhana's actions, he is appalled and horrified at what his son is doing. In the same way, when we see how much the ego is destroying our life, we can feel guilty and inadequate. We wish things could be different. Despite what we feel, the desire to change is not strong enough, so we continue to struggle.

Vidura's Attempts to Counsel Dhritarashtra – When Our Conscience Tries to Deliver Wisdom

Dhritarashtra is surrounded by men of nobility. His wise minister Vidura is always on hand to deliver words of advice. At every opportunity he warns Dhritarashtra of the consequences of failing in his duty. He tells him that if he does not intervene, then the upcoming war will bring about the destruction of everything he loves. Dhritarashtra hears the truth, but whenever there is a hope of doing anything right, Duryodhana and Shakuni enter and plead their case. Pathetically, the king cowers and turns his back on responsibility.

It becomes difficult to admit, but we actually know what we are doing. Just as Vidura never fails to point out the king's mistakes, our conscience never stops highlighting our flawed condition. We know what needs to be done, but the pull of the ego is just too strong. Like the king we have become an expert at cherry picking which ideas to implement and when. We are playing hide and seek with what we already know. We have buried the truth in the back of our minds and we are desperately trying not to look at it.

Despite Vidura being a servant, Dhritarashtra is actually scared of him. His words and prying eye are a constant threat. Every time he gives his opinion it is like an old wound getting pierced. There is no hiding for the king when Vidura is around. Likewise, when our conscience speaks, a mirror is created and we behold our reflection. We frantically try and resist seeing this image or at least pretend it is not as bad as it seems. One way to lessen the impact is to compare ourselves with other people. Everybody makes mistakes, we tell ourselves; nobody walks this path without making some significant errors. While that may be true, the ego specifically uses the idea to blow up the failings of others and makes our own mistakes seem comparatively normal.

When we are responsible, we do not draw such comparisons with others. We have our own bar that we have to reach, whether other people are failing or not is irrelevant. We know where we should be and we are honest about not hitting the mark. Rather than searching for ways to feel better about our mistakes we want to dialogue and learn so that we can find a way to improve. We welcome the possibility of someone contesting our worldview and pointing out our flaws. When Truth is of paramount importance, we do not protect the ego. Instead we are willing to hold ourselves up to the scrutiny of others.

Despite his fear, Dhritarashtra wants to keep Vidura by his side. So long as he is there, the king can convince himself that he is still on the side of righteousness. Although Vidura's words painfully cut to the core of his deception, they also act like a soothing balm. The king wants to favour his son, but at the same time he wants to be virtuous. By enquiring and listening to Vidura, at the most superficial level he feels he is still good. As long as Vidura keeps giving advice, the door to dharma is still open. Dhritarashtra does not have to walk through it, but at least it is there. Ultimately, he has no intention of implementing Vidura's instructions, because his loyalty is with Duryodhana.

Like the king, we also want to feel righteous. We are uncomfortable with the mistakes we have made and so in an effort to heal this, we try and find wisdom wherever we can. We talk to people who are kind and wise. We keep the company of those who seem exemplary in their devotion. We hope that by simply hanging around them we can make up for what we are doing. Repeatedly listening to good advice provides solace. Even if we do not implement any of it, it gives some kind of false assurance that we are still ok. We understand knowledge is no substitute for action, appreciation of the right thing cannot be the same as doing the right thing; but pearls of wisdom are comforting and keeping the company of good people makes us feel we are still somehow on track.

When Duryodhana misbehaves, Dhritarashtra summons Vidura. He pours out his heart, sometimes even confessing his mistakes. When the next chance comes to make amends, however, he fails to change course. We can often have periods of realisation where we clearly see our errors and what we have to do going forward. There is a resolve to change and start afresh. We have energy and enthusiasm. We make all kinds of big plans but somehow the ego manages to stop any of it becoming a reality.

Mere honesty of our faults cannot rectify the damage done by them. It is only action and the willingness to abandon the ego's desires that will set things right. There must be a determined effort to set the record straight.

The thing to realise is that our repeated lack of response carries a price. There comes a point when constant inaction eventually leads to our conscience disappearing altogether. Just as Duryodhana insults Vidura and causes him to leave, the ego gradually overrides our intuitive wisdom. Intuition is like a muscle; it needs to be used and listened to. Every time we fail to act on its insights, it weakens. Repeatedly ignoring what we know to be true, leads to our sense of discrimination disappearing altogether. Dhritarashtra imagined Vidura would always be there to serve him but he took his loyal servant for granted. In the same way, we can also fail to realise that the consistent refusal to change causes our inner wisdom to drift away.

Dhritarashtra's Bereavement – Realising that Life Waits for No One

Dhritarashtra does not value the privilege of sitting on the throne. He doesn't appreciate the rare honour of serving his kingdom and people. In the same way, when we decide to serve the ego, we forget that life is the grandest and most unique opportunity. There is so much to experience. We have abilities and wisdom that should be shared. We have the chance to serve and learn from others. Within each and every one of us there are divine blessings waiting to express themselves.

Duty is not about choosing what we want, when we want; it is about aligning ourselves with what life has called us to do. The ego makes us take everything for granted. We assume that we can spend years chasing our desires and then decide we are ready to fulfil our purpose when it suits us. But we cannot be part time seekers expecting full time blessings. Postponing our duty is postponing our journey to Truth. Irresponsibility wastes time. Months and years drift by and all the while we cannot see that the clock is ticking, and we are missing life.

The initial connection we felt at the beginning of our spiritual journey should be made to mature into a stable consistent joy that sustains our enthusiasm. Through disciplined and sincere focus, that first spark develops into a nourishing bond. It gets deeper and stronger. But when there is no effort or sacrifice, that stage never happens. Grace needs to be nurtured. The more we respond to it, the more it grows, and as it does, the level of responsibility needed to match it also increases. There comes a point when the connection we have received needs to be met with real transformation. If we fall behind the pace, like a wilting flower, we lose the inspiration to carry on. We start to wonder why we should bother being disciplined. Our mind becomes diverted and the ego convinces us to just relax and enjoy life. It is the easy option; the fruits are immediate, and we get to live on our terms.

Despite Dhritarashtra's innumerable mistakes, Krishna provides one more opportunity for him to be redeemed. In response to Duryodhana's threat He reveals His cosmic form which even Dhritarashtra, despite being blind, is blessed to see. Overwhelmed by Krishna's mercy, he cannot believe his good fortune. In the same way, even though we have wasted so much time, even though we have refused to take up responsibility, the Master is still willing to help us. He makes us aware that salvation is still available. At this late stage, He is ready to answer the call of our soul.

This is mercy. These blessings have not been earned. We have given almost nothing to this cause, but somehow the opportunity is still there. If we can take the Master's hand we will be pulled back onto our path and we will shake off the chains of the ego. When this happens, the service we attempted to run away from, is no longer seen as a burden. It becomes an honour, a treasure that we are eager to carry out. Through work and duty our relationship with the Divine gets stronger. When we look back, we can only bow our heads in gratitude at how much perseverance the Master had with us.

Often when we have not worked for grace however, we do not know how to value it. If we have been asleep for so long, then we become desensitised to what is unfolding before our eyes. Not only can this lead to taking life for granted, it can also lead to taking the Master for granted. This act of Krishna is a final attempt to avoid war. It is the last opportunity for Dhritarashtra to save his family from destruction. In the same way, the Master steps in when we are on the brink of falling away. If we are able to finally sever our attachment to our ego, then we can heed His words and steer ourselves away from the cliff edge. Through His grace, what looked like a wasted life can be transformed into one that becomes truly sanctified.

Life Lessons Rising Beyond the Hypocrisy of Dhritarashtra

- **Step Forward and Claim Your Spiritual Path**

  A cautious tentative approach will achieve very little on the spiritual path. Progress in any field requires clarity and bold determination. In the beginning we need time to learn and understand who we are and what we want. But at some point, if we are serious about changing, we have to give everything to this path. This does not mean all our flaws have to be eliminated or that we have to perfectly control our mind; but it does mean we need to firmly decide if realising the Divine is the centerpiece of our life or not.

  The ego's desire to withdraw and keep things as they are, should be challenged by boldly embracing change. We need to have the courage to step out of our comfort zone and challenge the normality of our life.

  If we hesitate and constantly weigh up what is worth our effort, we delay progress. Life is patient and will present multiple opportunities for us to grow. At the same time, if we miss the initial chance, we cannot expect the next opportunity to be as easy. The first chance for growth is the simplest and surest. It involves the least amount of difficulty. Transformation becomes steady and gradual. There are no gigantic leaps that have to be made, only a series of small steps to be taken. Little by little, we can feel we are coming closer to the goal. In short, the best way of dealing with the ego of Dhritarashtra is to take action immediately.

Practical Step: Whenever an opportunity is placed in front of you, try to ask 'Why not?' rather than 'Why should I?'. Unless there is a clear reason to turn a proposal down, take it up without delay.

• Embrace the Duty You Have Been Given

We often believe that living our purpose means experiencing boundless joy at every moment. Everyday should be filled with excitement and wonder. Because of this, when our job or role does not live up to our expectation, we imagine something has gone wrong. On the other hand, if we really believe we are on a path governed by grace, we see everything we are doing as divinely ordained. It has been handcrafted and given specifically to us for a reason. The fact that we are bored, stressed and frustrated with our situation does not dismiss this.

The job we are doing is meant to teach us something. There are things we have to work out and understandings we need to come to. There may well be a higher purpose that is waiting for us, but a higher purpose demands a higher state. In other words, we have to qualify ourselves first, and we do this by embracing what is in front of us. Only when we are at peace with our current situation can the next stage of our journey come about.

<u>Practical Step</u>: See the job or duty you are currently doing as being personally given and tailored for your advancement. Carry it out as if it were the only way you could spiritually progress.

- **Overcoming Laziness**

If we are lazy for God, God will be lazy for us. When we perform activities, we are acting out our relationship with the Divine. The intensity and quality of what we produce is a direct reflection of where we stand with Him. There has to be a striving in what we do, it is this effort which draws out what we have inside. It allows us to bring forth what is in our soul. Simply doing things for the sake of it does not qualify as doing our duty, we must work to manifest excellence. How much time we spend on something, how much attention to detail, how deeply we value our service, all reflect the level of devotion we have. Taking on challenges and inconveniences for a higher purpose strengthens our spiritual muscles and takes control away from the ego. Rather than being enslaved by it, we become the decision maker who steers the ship.

Rigid discipline also protects us from temptation and makes us less attracted to worldly things. Getting up early, delivering on our service and having a set time for spiritual practice are all important. Consistency in our routine provides an anchor for growth. Even if we have weaknesses and flaws, even if we are losing control in so many other parts of our life, we can still maintain order through habits and practices. This does not solve all our problems, but it does give some kind of stability. The maintenance of a disciplined life keeps the possibility for change available. Either we use action to build a spiritual fortress or succumb to laziness and create a playground for the ego to flourish.

If we are wise, we will understand that every act is a statement of cosmic significance. We will never trivialise or cheapen our service because we do not want to trivialise or cheapen our relationship with God.

Practical lesson: Wake up early even if you do not have to. Have set times for prayer and spiritual practice, treat these as appointments with the

Divine. Create deadlines for projects and rigidly keep to them. Do not make unrealistic goals that will never be reached. Everything you set out to do, should be seen as sacred promises that have to be fulfilled.

- **Self Analysis Must Lead to Transformation**

In the process of self-analysis, we may notice many issues and things that need addressing. This does not mean we can congratulate ourselves on simply acknowledging we have things to work on. Self-analysis has to produce results, and by results we mean transformation. Our progress must be measured by what we can physically notice such as changes in our routine and how we carry out our duties.

Practical Step: Measure your development by external outcomes. Have your habits changed? Are you saying 'yes' to opportunities? Are you attending and delivering all that you are required to do? Is your talent being maximised for a higher purpose? Ask people whom you trust if they have noticed a change and take their analysis seriously.

- **Value the Master's Presence**

The presence of the Master in our life is a clear sign that the goal of our path can be attained. It is not some pipe dream that we are aspiring for, but a real possibility. Therefore, the Master's teachings cannot be brushed to one side. Even if they are inconvenient, His instructions have to be implemented as if everything depended on it.

The closer we are to the Divine, the greater the responsibility. We have to realise that beneath the normality of daily living, a cosmic situation is unfolding. If the Master holds out His hand, it means life has faith in us. It trusts that we can take the right steps. Unlike Dhritarashtra, we need to recognise this mercy and be ready to drop everything to take it.

<u>Practical Step</u>: Never compromise on the Master's instruction. Take care that you are not reinterpreting or diluting His wishes to suit your preferences. Carry out any direction immediately and as accurately as possible. Do not procrastinate.

Gandhari – The Hypocrisy of Resentment

All Gandhari could hear was the uncontrollable wailing of women. She gripped her maidservant's hand tightly as she was led through the battlefield. The scene was being described to her as she manoeuvred in between the endless rows of corpses. There were decapitated bodies, severed limbs and rivers of blood. Her thoughts were being drowned by agonising shouts of wives calling out their husband's names, and mothers beating their chests over their dead sons. Here she was no queen, she had no status. She was just another woman who had lost everything.

Many years ago, she was the young princess of Gandhar eagerly looking forward to her marriage. She had heard her husband was handsome, she had been told that he possessed immense strength, and then, at the eleventh hour, she also learned that he had been blind since birth. The shocking news shattered her expectations. In an instant the perfect life she had dreamt of for so long had all completely vanished. Even though she was deeply wounded, she did not react, she did not rebel or protest. Strangely Gandhari showed no emotion. Her husband was her lord no matter what, and she would follow him to the ends of the Earth unconditionally. Her job was to serve him and be his rock in every situation.

But so long as she had her sight, there was no chance of serving him for she would be his superior. He would have to look to her as an authority, she would end up ruling the kingdom while her husband watched on. How would that make him feel? He would be humiliated. He would lose the respect of his ministers and subjects all because of her. No, she would not allow it.

That fateful day, she took upon herself the most extreme of vows. Gandhari looked up one last time and said goodbye to the world. She took a piece of cloth and tied it across her eyes. If her husband lived in darkness, then so would she. This would be her gift to him, her offering to their marriage.

This was just the beginning of many more sacrifices. Gandhari remembered how she remained pregnant for two long years. Her frustration reached boiling point when the news of Kunti's new son reached her. Her child's claim to the throne could well trump that of Gandhari's own children. In

a fit of rage, she ordered the foetus to be beaten out of her, and out came a ball of flesh. The whole palace was horrified. Sage Vyasa ordered it to be divided into a hundred parts, and from each one a son was born.

From the beginning she always knew her children were unrighteous, and Duryodhana was the worst of them, but they were hers, and her love for them never wavered. Gandhari did her best to bring them up in the right way, but their vile selfishness paved the way for their death. Now she had to walk amongst the dead bodies hearing the names of each of her hundred sons as they were called out to her.

The Pandavas came and stood to offer their respects. What could be said to the nephews who had just killed her children? She interrogated Bhima as to why he could not have left just one of her sons alive. Even though listening to his reply nearly destroyed her, Gandhari restrained her anger. Later Krishna Himself came seeking blessings. She knew He was no ordinary mortal, the sages had declared He was a divine incarnation, God Himself. If He was Divine then how could He have let this happen? Krishna was on the battlefield, He witnessed the terrible slaughter and bloodshed. He was the one who could have stopped this catastrophe and the horrific suffering. He watched as one family annihilated itself. The more she thought about it, the more enraged she became.

137

Not only had this divine personality stood by, He had orchestrated the whole saga. From behind the scenes Krishna had been directing everything. He didn't want peace, He never did. His superficial righteous preaching was all just a cover up. The unbearable grief at the loss of her sons, the wounds of all the women, the tragedy of the whole situation began to overwhelm her. How could He stand by and watch such suffering? Why did He have to go so far? There must have been another way. As she listened to Krishna's pacifying words, she felt deceived. It all became clear: He had been playing her all along, all of this was His fault. Trembling with fury and with every ounce of power she could muster, Gandhari unleashed a curse. The same devastation that had befallen her family would happen to Krishna. Just as her family had destroyed itself, the Yadava family too would kill each other and Krishna Himself would lose His life. Upon uttering these words Gandhari, drained of all her energy, collapsed on the floor in a pitiful mess.

Dhritarashtra's Blindness Destroys Gandhari's Dreams – When Life Stops Us Fulfilling Our Desires

It is normal to begin the spiritual path with enthusiasm. When everything is new, we are full of anticipation for what lies ahead. Like the beginning of a romance, everything is vibrant and exciting. With eagerness we look forward to walking this new road of self-discovery. Gandhari too begins with the same excitement. She is about to get married to a great and noble prince.

He is handsome, strong and is part of one of the greatest kingdoms – what more could a princess want? But the news that he is blind rocks her whole world. In an instant everything she envisaged about her perfect marriage collapses.

The discovery of Dhritarashtra's blindness is a cruel turn of events for Gandhari. She is both innocent and naïve, and has yet to experience any real suffering. When we have grown up in a comfortable way, we do not know the harsh nature of life. It can deliver shocking blows that ruin all that we take for granted. When we have lived relatively well, it is easy to build hopes and develop plans that we assume will be fulfilled. When everything so far has worked out, why wouldn't the rest of our life play out in a similar way? Of course, we know tragedy happens, we understand that awful things go on all the time, but inside we do not believe they will ever happen to us. Our purpose is to be happy; life is here to make our dreams come true.

Gandhari's marriage stands for the first major incident that forces us to recognise that we cannot have our own way. We see, for example, that the relationship we dreamed of is not going to happen, or it becomes clear that the successful career we hoped for will not materialise. On the spiritual path there may be specific expectations that we now recognise cannot be attained. In our minds we had a life plan, we had specific things we wanted to achieve. But when the desires we desperately want are not granted, it is a huge wake up call. We realise that life is not about running from one pleasurable experience to another. Superficially, it is an obvious point, but internally it is a disturbing revelation. Immediately we are forced to stop and take stock. The script we believed our life was supposed to stick to has to be torn up. If we cannot have what we want, if things are not going to follow our plan, how should we carry on?

When crisis strikes, the door is wide open for spiritual growth. In fact, it is an opportunity for a quantum leap. The old, false conceptions that we have clung to can be cast aside. The identity that we have become attached to can be let go of. It is a chance to embrace a new direction. We can shift from running after mundane happiness to developing a deeper meaning for why we exist. Crises are an initiation into a new way of life. It is difficult to stomach, and it requires immense courage to rise to the opportunity. But if we can do it, we will be reborn.

To make this leap, there has to be a sincere acceptance of what has happened. When life is calling us to take a major shift in perspective, we need to make peace with what has been thrown our way. However much we have lost, tragedy needs to be seen as part of a larger plan. With the right wisdom, we will understand that everything is happening for a reason. We may not fully comprehend it, but we can still trust in a divine plan. Gandhari however fails to do this. The prospect of having a blind husband is too big a hurt to deal with. She feels betrayed by life. As a princess she has staked all her happiness on marriage and now it has been robbed from her. The mountain is too big to climb.

If the ego stops us accepting what has happened, then it becomes difficult to adopt a higher perspective. Going forward there are essentially two options: Either we protest, openly wearing our wounds on our sleeve, telling the world of the injustices we have suffered; or we bury the hurt, conceal it as best we can, and pretend to embrace our new situation. Gandhari does the latter. She does not want the world to know the pain she is in. Despite all she is feeling, she wants to maintain a sense of duty and do the 'right' thing. It does not matter what burden she has to bear; it does not matter if all she has ever wanted has been thrown to the ground, now is not the time for self-indulgence, she has to be strong, stoic and resilient.

On the surface this sounds like an admirable thing

to do. In this case however, Gandhari is not being honest. Her determined attitude has not come from a genuine acceptance of her situation, it is being used as a distraction from her turmoil. She cannot see it, but she is lying to herself.

In the same way, when the ego is hurt, we can also feel like we have to power through. Somehow, we must find a way to cover up the disappointment and regret at not achieving our aspirations. The world must not know how badly we have been affected, but most of all, we ourselves must not know, and so we take a deep breath and push all our issues as far down as we can. Out of sight, out of mind. Now we look forward and see what needs to be done. We think we have moved on, but all the while this suppression makes us uneasy. We are not happy, and we know it, but somehow we have to be. By sheer force of will, we must make this ok. To do this we need to go over and above a normal reaction and overcompensate. We cannot simply be ok with things we have to pretend to be excited and full of energy. We have to show everyone including ourselves that we have come to terms with our situation. In other words, we have to be dishonest and act like things are not just good, but wonderful.

Gandhari Ties Her Blindfold – When Virtue Is Used to Hide Resentment

The ego of Gandhari is very specific. When we do not get the things we want either spiritually or materially,

142

we feel hurt. At the same time we know that the right thing to do is accept what has happened. Consequently we pressure ourselves to keep going. We carry on with our path. But all the while, unknown to us, we harbor a belief that life or God has forced us to take this road.

The need to fake an acceptance of what has happened is what makes Gandhari take the extreme act of blindfolding herself. She believes it is a sign of virtue, but really it is a sign of desperation. Likewise, in an effort to rise above the hurt of our ego, we can end up diving headfirst into all manner of responsibilities. We throw ourselves into intense service. Without a second thought we give up all that we love and adopt the most difficult and thankless of jobs. The moment one thing is finished, we jump to the next. We are always the first to arrive and the last to leave. We are restless, constantly feeling we have to do more. In our minds, we have an idea of holiness and we are striving to act it out. People marvel at how well we are doing and how much we have taken on, and this encourages us even more. To the innocent bystander it looks like we are a model servant.

The reality is there is little virtue here, but the beginnings of resentment. Far from being based on devotion, our actions are founded on the injustice which has been thrown at us. The ego's broken dreams are still buried deep within us and we are trying to cover it with excessive, false enthusiasm. Outwardly we act with tremendous passion, but internally we have grown to dislike the whole situation we are in. In our hearts we still want our old life plan to manifest.

Just like Gandhari is under pressure to be the dutiful wife, we too feel the burden of having to live up to what it means to be on a spiritual path. We ignore our negative emotions and adopt a heroic zeal. We brush all our issues to one side, roll up our sleeves and get stuck in. While our actions look pious, much of what we do does not come from a peaceful, secure place. It is fuelled by a bitterness for the situation we have found ourselves in. Although we have chosen this path, somehow deep inside we feel like we have been pushed into it.

When we truly accept a situation, there is no need to take drastic action. We are happy with where we are in life, there is no resentment but rather contentment. We are at peace and everything we do is done with genuine love. We are not restless, but measured and grounded. We do not have to prove anything to ourselves or anyone else. The challenges we went through are perceived as a blessing, something that opened the door to where we are today. We see that the things we were desperately clinging on to would have held us back. If anything we are grateful for not having them fulfilled.

When we have not accepted our life, balanced discrimination can end up being replaced with fiery emotions. A large part of us is holding onto old dreams, and another part is bullying us to try and be a model person. For now, we choose to be good and devoted. But the lack of reconciliation between the two, means our spiritual path is always in tension.

Gandhari says she is blindfolding herself for the welfare of her husband, but if she really wanted to serve him, she could have been his eyes. She could have been that strength that he relied upon to rule the kingdom. The vow to never see light again did nothing to help Dhritarashtra. In fact, it added another burden. The truth is that Gandhari's immense act was not one of service, it was an expression of her resentment.

Similarly, if we still feel life has been unjust, the ego can use service as a form of self-indulgence. We cannot go round telling people of our grievances, so we find another way to do this, one that makes us look like the martyr. The aim is to gain attention, to make people feel sorry for us. The beauty of playing this role is that our pain becomes an opportunity to gain praise and honour. Because we have disguised it so well, our hurt becomes respected, even adored by others. Somehow, we have managed to transform the shattering of our dreams into an opportunity for veneration. The sympathy of others becomes a great source of comfort. By displaying our sacrifice, we can end up creating something quite enjoyable. The ego makes us happily play the victim and feel pity for ourselves.

If we are truly sincere, we will not give in to this kind of indulgence. We do not want the attention of others.

Our solace and strength come from the Divine. This does not mean we do not seek advice. There are always times when other people can support and help, but when we do turn to them, we have no interest in their sympathy. We do not want others to feel sorry for us because we do not feel sorry for ourselves. When we know the Divine is present in our lives, there is no place for victimhood.

Gandhari Gives Birth to the Kauravas – Resentment Allows the Ego to Take Centre Stage

As time goes on, the chance to fulfil our previous desires drifts further away. We have forced ourselves (or rather we feel like life has) to renounce personal enjoyment and stick to what we believe is right, but still we are not at peace. The denial and dishonesty of what we truly want eventually pushes the ego to the surface. That which has been controlling things in the background now takes centre stage. When Gandhari hears about Kunti's first child, she is filled with frustration at her condition. She orders the foetus within her to be beaten out and then Duryodhana and the rest of the Kauravas come to life.

The birth of her children is where the ego and all our insecurities start to rise up. Before we were just absorbed in our own misfortune, but now we look up and everybody else appears happier and more successful. Just as Gandhari is envious of Kunti, we feel the same when we see those around being given everything that we want. What we have been refused, appears to be readily granted to everyone else. Everywhere people seem to have achieved their spiritual goals, they have great relationships, wealth and success.

Whenever we see someone enjoying the life we hoped for, we might say how much we are pleased for them, but there is a part of us hoping it all falls apart. Behind our superficial, cheery exterior, the ego makes us jealous and it does not wish them well. Such comparisons often make us doubt what we are doing. When there are so many examples of other people who have fulfilled their dreams, we question if we were right to even walk this path.

 Gandhari is not like her husband, she does not indulge Duryodhana. She is fully aware that he is a tyrant who will only bring disaster. At the same time, he is her son, and she cannot turn her back on him. She too wants to see him on the throne, but so far, not at the cost of righteousness. While Dhritrashtra quietly paves the way for Duryodhana to get his way, Gandhari stands against him. Although she is doing the right thing, she is torn. She is trying to follow dharma, but within her she desperately wants her son to be king.

It is the same for us, even though our perceived injustice creates intense pressure within us, we do not want to give up on our principles. The ego cannot be allowed to dictate things. We want to be good. We know how a good person ought to be and as much as possible we want to live up to that. Carrying on with our duty is the most important thing. We will not let this situation overcome us; the suppression of our aspirations must continue.

In many ways, this is the right attitude to have. The worst thing we can do is stop serving and carrying out the role we have been given. Performing our duty maintains our connection with our path. Working as selflessly as possible has the potential to purify and help us rise above the issues which are holding us back. Service and taking up responsibility, however, is not a magic solution that can cure us of this condition. It can inspire and keep us moving forward, but unless we come to terms with what we do not have, life will always be a struggle. We can distract ourselves with work and entertainment, but if we have not risen beyond these desires, as each day passes things only get harder.

On the surface it appears as if the dam is holding strong, but behind it there is chaos. The dishonesty we carry makes us have major mood swings. One minute we are stable and ready to serve, the next we are retreating into a cave unable to face the world. Whenever we are praised or given what we want, we have moments of relief. The ego is fed, and life becomes more tolerable. The longer we go trying to selflessly perform our duty, the more we have to pretend to play the humble servant, the more taxing the situation gets. As time goes on, the ego's dominance makes it increasingly difficult to ignore; we can no longer act out the role of a good spiritual seeker. The same demands become heavier and our ability to power through gets weaker.

Growth happens when we make inner development the centre of our lives. This is the attitude that gives us strength and determination; we are not swayed by doubts or plagued by material desires. We know what our aim is, and we are clear about what we have to do.

But right from the very beginning the ego has stopped us developing this resolve. Because we have not been completely honest with what we want, we become weak. We cannot discover that inner resilience. The ego makes us wonder what might have been had we stuck to chasing our previous goals. Maybe we would have been happier, perhaps we could have avoided this suffering. Gradually part of us starts to really entertain the possibility of throwing in the towel and choosing a different road.

Along with this perspective the ego has a habit of attaching to other people who are also going through similar issues. They seem to understand our pain. The shared sense of victimhood can create a kind of club. Here we have the chance to talk about our problems and struggles.

Unfortunately, these friendships are not built on a desire to help one another grow spiritually, but on the ego's enjoyment of self-pity. The discussions are rarely driven

149

to finding a solution, but to validate our suffering. We indulge the other person and they in turn indulge us. It is easy to believe we are helping one another, but in truth we are propping up each other's negativity. The group provides an audience who are ready to delight and applaud our drama. It takes us away from real self-reflection and instead makes us enjoy the problems which have come to define our path.

Eventually the Kauravas come face to face with the Pandavas on the battlefield. Bhima is unstoppable, and as each day passes, Gandhari hears the news that more of her sons have been killed. Now all her worst fears are being released. There is nowhere to turn. The death of the Kauravas marks the point, where the issues we have been experiencing become too intense. We cannot enjoy being self-indulgent. There is no reason to try and be that perfect spiritual seeker. It is no longer worth trying to prove our holiness.

Slowly the realisation dawns on us that we will never realise our ego's desires. All the happiness and success we longed for will never be experienced. Deep down, we secretly nurtured a hope that maybe, just maybe we might attain them one day, or at least somehow it would all come good. Now that hope has gone. No matter what happens Duryodhana is not going to sit on the throne. We do not see that maybe this could all be a blessing in disguise. It could be an opportunity for something much greater. Instead we feel as if we have ventured too far down this road, and we have given up too much, now we have missed the chance for happiness.

Gandhari Blesses Duryodhana – When the Ego Is No Longer Suppressed

Finally, we realise all the sacrifice we endured was ultimately for nothing. We have given everything to the path, we have done all that was asked of us, but still we are unhappy. The ego does not want to understand why this has happened. It will not allow us to see that right from the start our motivation was not to serve something higher and realise our true potential; we were trying to cover up the resentment we felt. This is what has brought about this rageful state.

As the horrific war draws to a close, Gandhari breaks down. Ninety-nine of her beloved sons have been killed by Bhima. Finally, she renounces the virtuous lady she once was. In an effort to keep her last son Duryodhana alive, she breaks her vow. Removing her blindfold, she looks upon him for the first time and empowers him with an impenetrable armour.

Just as the loss of Gandhari's sons is too much to bear, the perceived injustice we have had to put up with is overwhelming. The ego cannot stand by and watch our desires and dreams being taken from us. We can no longer be heroically righteous about how we feel. Subconsciously we assumed that if we ran this out for long enough, there would be some reward, that it would all correct itself. Now we see that the big payoff is not going to happen and our frustration erupts forth. Just as Gandhari's motherly instincts can no longer be buried behind her righteous character, we can no longer deny the ego's demands.

Gandhari's blessing of Duryodhana is the point where we give in and allow the ego to have its way. We are tired of being good, tired of being the valiant hero, so it is time to unleash who we are. All the piety we displayed is thrown aside and replaced with a ferocious persona that wants to make its mark. Instead of being the humble servant at the back, we push ourselves forward and take control.

We are not interested in bowing down and stepping aside, we instead enforce what we want. The praise of others is irrelevant, because everything has been denied to us already. It is time to make up for lost time. This is where we grab and steal whatever is available. We must now make ourselves the priority above all other things. Duryodhana has to win this war and our ego must have its way. We do not care about trying to be humble or attaining some lofty goal of self-realisation, we want a revolution that gives us power. Finally, we can breathe a sigh of relief; our defiance is liberating. We have given up playing the role of a suffering saint, we are now an empowered warrior out for justice. In a truly rebellious mood, we move from a life of service to a life of vengeance.

The victim complex makes us speak out. We are not going to hide who we are anymore, anyone who stands in our way is our enemy. Every time we are asked to do something, we see it as some kind of violation. The ego makes us believe we are being exploited and controlled by others. We feel we are being utilised for other people's profit. Instead of opportunities we see potential traps, where individuals are trying to manipulate us. The mind has a way of completely warping reality, nobody can make us see sense, not even the Master. When He stretches out His hand, we do not trust it and when He offers us advice, we cannot listen.

Gandhari Blames Krishna – When the Ego Makes us Turn Against the Master

Despite the protection Gandhari has given

Duryodhana, he is eventually defeated. There is only so long the ego's crusade can survive. When we are on a spiritual path everything eventually gets called out. Our revolution has been short lived and instead of a dramatic change, we have run into a brick wall. The ego pushed for its survival as long as it could, but finally we see after all our frustrated effort, we have achieved nothing.

When Gandhari hears the wails of the other women, she experiences the full impact of this terrible war. The tragic loss that she and many thousands of others have suffered cause her to lose any sense of self-restraint. When Krishna approaches, she recognises that He is the Lord, the supreme controller. He is the one who could have saved her sons, the one who could have prevented the horror of this war. Because of Him the entire battlefield is soaked in blood. When she turns to Krishna, Gandhari's rage only increases.

The Master is the Divine, He is Life. Because we believe fate has been so harsh to us, naturally He becomes the scapegoat where we pin all our woes. The emotional turmoil of not getting what we want requires an outlet. The ego needs something, someone, to take responsibility for the way our life has turned out. When we can see the Divinity of the Master, but we cannot see His wisdom or purpose, the ego treats Him as an omnipotent being with human intentions. It perceives Him as the cruellest and most heartless of personalities. We cannot understand why anybody with compassion could standby and not save us from all these difficulties. Instead of harbouring gratitude to the Master and to life, we turn them into enemies that we are at war with.

However, like Krishna, the physical form of the Master has done nothing directly. In fact, in the same way that Krishna came on a peace mission to help Duryodhana, the Master repeatedly attempted to guide us. He did everything to set our mind in the right direction, but the ego refused to listen. Life will wait for us to change, but there is a limit to its patience. When no steps are being taken, it organises itself to set the record straight.

On the surface Krishna is just the innocent charioteer of Arjuna, but in reality, He is responsible for the destruction of the Kauravas; as the Supreme Lord He has orchestrated the whole affair. Similarly, on a physical level, the Master has hardly been involved in our life, but we intuitively know he has had everything to do with it. Behind the scenes He has controlled events to bring us to this point. The various scenarios have not happened by chance but by design. Nature has worked things into perfect alignment for us to face what is needed.

Gandhari's suffering has clouded her perception. She fails to accept that Duryodhana's fate was inevitable. Krishna has come to uphold dharma, and this inevitably means the destruction of her sons. While she sees that He is in control, she has no appreciation of what His Divine plan is. Similarly, we too do not comprehend what the goal of our spiritual path is and what the Master has come to do. When we embark on this journey to Truth, His job is to reveal our divine self to us. This means seeing both the positive and negative. It means recognising our limitation and rising above it, it involves facing our ego and renouncing it. Real spirituality is not a life of quiet contemplation and inner peace, it is about core, irreversible transformation.

If we have the proper vision, we will see what has happened as a sign of unconditional Love. The Master is prepared to go to any lengths to remove our ego. He will sacrifice His name and reputation just so we can grow. However much negativity we have, He will do whatever is necessary to rid us of it. When Truth is what we want, we rejoice when we see how far the Master is willing to go for our sake. All the challenges we have had to endure are actually a sign that the Divine longs for us. Life has organised various situations to bring us to this point. It means we are cared for. We have not been allowed to drown in worldly desires. The fact that we have had no choice is actually a sign of grace. If all other doors have been closed, then the Divine becomes the only option. That is what our soul has been wanting all along.

The truth is, unless we are sincere, we cannot adopt this perspective. While clinging to her son, Gandhari always forced herself to be righteous. In the same way, the ego has made us live a lie. We have pretended to be loyal to our path while subconsciously holding on to other desires. We have deceived ourselves throughout this whole process. Because we were so stuck on life being the way we wanted it, there was no room for spiritual progress, there was no room to fulfil our purpose. We should have made peace with our old aspirations instead of suppressing feelings and pretending to be dedicated. Ultimately, the reason we feel cheated is because we have been cheating ourselves.

The Curse of Gandhari – How The Ego Makes Us Bitter

When we are heavily invested in a victim mentality, any idea of taking responsibility for our negative emotions is seen as incredibly offensive. Like with Duryodhana, we do not want to be humble and bow to the situation.

We know that if we do come to terms with not fulfilling our expectations, it will eventually lead us back to the Master's feet. We will see that our reaction is wrong, we will recognise a higher perspective, we will go within, and inevitably we will have to accept that life was always working for our own good. This is something the ego cannot let happen. Clinging to negativity is its strength.

As a result, we go on believing we have a right to feel hurt. 'How can any of this be our fault?' We ask. Far from recognising the negativity we carry, the ego can even become self-righteous. In order to vindicate our position, it casts everyone else as superficial and fake. It tells us that we are the one who is sincere, and this is why we stand out amongst the crowd. We are not being self-indulgent, we are the only ones courageous enough to stand for truth. We are led to believe we are fighting for what is right in a world which is drowning in deceit.

The curse of Gandhari allows the ego to blame the Master and still play the victim. The whole drama is placed upon His head. The apparent injustice we have endured needs some kind of relief. The ego turns its bitterness upon the Master and against all those who support Him. We have our story, we have the justification needed. So, with our head held high, we stomp off to explore a new life. Just as Krishna happily receives the curse and moves on, the Master takes our negativity and remains unperturbed.

Life Lessons Rising Beyond the Hypocrisy of Gandhari

- **Choose Growth over Happiness**

    Almost everyone defines success by getting what they want, when they want. The problem with this is that it is out of touch with reality. Life is never going to give us everything we hope for, and rarely does it fulfil even most of our wish list. A plan for happiness is potentially a plan for unhappiness.

    If we have a rigid life strategy that we are deeply attached to, we will be waiting for disappointment. Having spiritual growth as a goal over happiness is to place inner development over pleasure. It is an attitudinal shift where we understand there is a greater reason to live than trying to fulfil a superficial life plan. This does not guarantee that things will always be joyful as tragedy can strike at any moment, but it does give us the tools to deal with the complexities we are likely to face.

    Living a life defined by inner growth does not stop us taking opportunities to be happy, but it does provide a degree of detachment. We are not completely defined by whether or not we have achieved specific goals. When things do not go to plan, we are able to find another space inside ourselves that can cope and forge a different way forward. If we are to walk a spiritual path, aspiring for meaning over happiness is essential. Truth carries ultimate meaning, while the ego is out for vain pleasure; the two are diametrically opposed.

<u>Practical Step</u>: Train your mind to redefine success. As much as possible, avoid being fixated with achieving specific things in your life. Put aside any ideas of how and when things should be delivered to you. Life is a blank canvas, an adventure, so be open to everything and anything that might happen. Trust that all events are part of a bigger plan that is yet to reveal itself.

- **Beware of Unconscious Expectation**

In an effort to become a good devotee we can try and be as dutiful and disciplined as possible. We must be cautious however, as there is a danger of acting too quickly. We have to be careful about being motivated by ungrounded hype. Making big commitments whilst failing to address our desires can lead to expectation. Because we have given up or lost out on what we really want, subconsciously we can end up expecting our spiritual path to compensate us. We can believe that the happiness we gave up has to be returned to us in some way.

If this does not happen, we can start to feel bitter.

160

Whenever things get tough, this will grow and eventually dominate everything. Unless we put these issues to bed, there will always be part of us wondering what could have been. Our time will not be spent on sincerely advancing, but wasted on weighing up whether we have made the right decision to even be on this path.

<u>Practical Step</u>: At no point should you stop or delay serving on the spiritual path. But as early and as often as possible, it is important to ask whether you carry unfulfilled aspirations or a sense of injustice for what you might have missed out on. Do not bury these desires, look at them. Weigh up how important they are to you. Ask yourself if you are strong enough to move past them, or do they need to be pursued?

- **Do Not Enjoy Self-Pity**

When things do not go our way, the easiest thing to do is withdraw and sulk. It is comforting and cosy. Although self-pity is tempting, it is dangerous. Not only does it stop us turning inwards, it can encourage us to turn against our path. It is the ego's way of enticing us into its world. If we feel sorry for ourselves for too long, it can easily turn into resentment.

Whenever troubles come, it is natural to take time out to reflect and recover. We cannot force ourselves to be perfectly strong in all situations. At the same time, the situation cannot be abused for enjoyment. There is nothing wrong in discussing our difficulties with others, it is often very healthy, but there must be a point to such discussions. At all times we have to be looking for solutions and a higher understanding that aligns us with our purpose.

Spiritual association should be about a collection of like-minded individuals who are dedicated to advancing, not a group of people who enjoy discussing their hurt. The company we keep should help us rise out of our situation as quickly as possible and not perpetuate it. When faced with difficulties we need to take the time we need, but we have to take a stand when the ego is dragging us into self-indulgence.

Practical Step: If difficulties come, then get some distance and perspective. But use this opportunity to change your mindset to a positive one. Think about the many blessings you have received. See how fortunate you are compared to so many others. Appreciate what you have and the people you have encountered. They have all led to where you are now. Make these sentiments stronger than the negative emotions which might allow you to play the victim.

- **Overcoming Resentment**

If we find ourselves feeling resentment, as difficult as it might be, we should acknowledge that this is simply our ego stomping its feet. We need to understand that the spiritual path is not a democracy where we can vote for what we want to happen.

Life will not wrong us, but it will reflect us. In some way, the circumstances we are in are displaying a truth that we need to take notice of. The humbler we are, the more wisdom we can draw out of the situation. Like following a treasure trail, if we can work out the signs, we can get to the root of why we are where we are.

Fundamentally we have to trust that there is an unseen hand at work directing events. Resentment can then be transformed into an opportunity. If we trust that our life is guided, then in every problem there is the solution. The true measure of whether we have risen above bitterness is that instead of having regrets, we only have gratitude. The challenges we have endured must eventually be looked upon as wonderful blessings that we would never want to change.

Practical Step: Rather than asking 'Why me?' we should try and ask 'What do I have to learn? What changes is this situation calling me to make?'

Realise that the harsher the lesson, the more Life is longing for you to evolve. At some level you have invoked this to grow. Humbly meditate on the circumstances you are in, because within it, there is a profound teaching and the way forward.

Shakuni – The Hypocrisy of Cunningness

'Seven!' Shakuni looked down at the dice. Yet again he had drawn the right number at precisely the right time. Duryodhana punched the air in a state of euphoria while Dushasana laughed uncontrollably. The atmosphere was charged, shouts and groans were erupting from all sides of the gambling hall. Yudhishthira sat in a state of shock, almost numb to everything that was happening. His eyes were transfixed on the dice which had robbed him of his kingdom. Bhima and the other Pandavas wept in frustration. They were held hostage by their obedience. There was no way they could contest their elder brother and so they sat tearing out their hair.

The elders of the court, Bhishma, Drona and Kripacharya also kept a deathly silence while they witnessed the tragedy unfolding. Shakuni had won every time. Yudhishthira had lost his wealth, kingdom, brothers and now himself to Duryodhana. In just a few throws, these mighty rulers had been reduced to slaves. Shakuni breathed a sigh of relief. He had delivered everything his nephew had been pining for. He gave a dastardly smile, at last he could bask in the knowledge that Duryodhana's enemies would be destroyed.

The blindfolding of Gandhari had a profound effect on Shakuni. The loss and humiliation transformed him. Marrying his sister to a blind king was an insult to his family. Who did the Kurus think they were? It was this injustice that made him dedicate his whole life to his nephew. Duryodhana had to take the throne one way or another. There was no room for compromise, all obstacles and enemies had to be eradicated. He leaned on Dhritarashtra and gave him the stories he needed. Ultimately the king wanted the same thing, to see his son rule the kingdom. He just needed the right reasoning to make it happen. This is where Shakuni came into his own. His cunning insight was second to none.

When it came to virtue and wisdom, Yudhishthira was the most respected of all. Duryodhana possessed none of the qualifications to rule, nor did he have the might to vanquish his enemies head on, but what he lacked in military prowess, Shakuni made up for in political tact. The Pandavas had Krishna as their councillor. To win this game, there needs to be a willingness to bend the rules and know what you can get

166

away with. There was no doubt Krishna was powerful and intelligent, but Shakuni doubted whether He had enough intelligence to match him. Within his mind, he felt he had the upper hand.

The whole kingdom was filled with righteous personalities and Dhritarashtra was forced to appease them. Shakuni's art of deception meant he could always manoeuvre a way forward. His plans lay just beyond the objection of Bhishma and Vidura. His devious strategies gave enough cover to legally vanquish the Pandavas. This was the gift that Shakuni brought to the Kauravas.

'Let us keep playing!' shouted Duryodhana. Yudhishthira looked somewhat perplexed; he had already lost everything, including himself, so how could the game carry on? "I want Draupadi! Uncle, make it happen!" Shakuni gave a sly grin and once again picked up the dice.

Shakuni Serves Duryodhana – How the Ego Develops Cunningness on the Spiritual Path

Duryodhana wants to conquer his enemies and it is his uncle's job to make it happen. With Shakuni, nothing he does is what it seems; there is always an ulterior motive behind every action. Life is like a chess game, where every move is calculated for a reason. Whereas Dhritarashtra's actions bring him guilt and conflict, Shakuni is perfectly happy to use any amount of trickery and dishonesty to make Duryodhana rule.

There is a reason why Shakuni has this bond with

Duryodhana. From the beginning, the marriage of Gandhari to a blind king humiliated him. His sister was both beautiful and devout, and deserved the best king in the land, but the pressure of the Kuru clan forced his father to give her away. The decision to plunge herself into darkness alongside her husband was another dagger to Shakuni's heart. Somehow, he has to make amends for this insult, he knows that Gandhari's terrible sacrifice can only be reconciled through Duryodhana. If his nephew can grab the throne, then this injustice can be set right.

Just as he is anxious to rectify his family's humiliation, we too can have a need to set the record straight. Somewhere inside us we feel we have been wronged or not given enough respect. This may be due to a particular incident, or something that stretches right back to our childhood. Either way, we have a point to prove, we are looking to achieve something and show what we are capable of. Sometimes we want to shine and excel in our service, other times we want to impress or even control people. When it comes to the spiritual path the ego puts progress to one side. Having the approval of people around us becomes our goal. Rather than dedicating ourselves to inner work, the ego is deviously looking for some kind of shortcut to gaining recognition.

As we have seen with Dhritarashtra, the ego can often slyly use excuses to avoid doing our duty. Shakuni also carries a similar deviousness, but instead of using it to retreat away from the world, it seeks to actively engage in it on behalf of the ego. Duryodhana uses his father for protection but uses his uncle to try and get what he wants. This aspect of the ego is calculated and intelligent. Its cunningness bends the rules and reinterprets our principles to get its way. This is not necessarily a state that we live from all the time. It is a mode, a certain attitude we pick up whenever we want something. Like Shakuni, within the boundaries of what is acceptable, the ego tries to shine and fulfil its ambitions.

Shakuni Plots to Defeat the Pandavas – When the Ego Tries to Compete with Others

Shakuni knows how to use Dhritarashtra to get things done, he understands how to play palace politics with Vidura and Bhishma. In the same way, when the ego wants attention and recognition, naturally other people become our focus. Sometimes they are seen as useful allies that can help us get what we are looking for, other times they can be viewed as some kind of threat to what we want. As mentioned, this is not a condition we always live from. In our hearts we may still have a genuine desire to grow and transform, but alongside this we carry insecurities and desires which change our mindset and behaviour. When we are keen to be noticed, we end up becoming like a teenager at school, constantly assessing our social status. Our attention shifts to how popular and respected we are. We wonder if people are praising what we are doing. Even more than ourselves, we want to know how well others are doing.

Just as Shakuni is forever conspiring for Duryodhana,

the ego makes us intensely interested in other people's business. Our ear is to the ground ready to receive the latest information. We want to know who is making progress and who is failing. We are keen to find out which individuals are close to the Master and what blessings they have received. Are people impressed or critical of what they are doing? When there is any kind of incident or scandal, we are alert to the details and are quick to whisper them into the ears of others. The ego puts us on surveillance. We listen, calculate and gather as much information as possible.

It can be possible to have an interest in these things for the right reasons. Observing what other people do can provide useful lessons. We can understand what pitfalls to avoid and how certain traits take us in different directions. This however, is not the reason why our ego is involved. It wants to know these things, because it enjoys the drama. Like watching a soap opera, it provides entertainment. We enjoy juicy gossip and the highs and lows people have to face.

But perhaps more than this, we want to compare where we stand. We have a particular eye on individuals who carry out similar roles to us. These are our rivals, the people who might eclipse our glory. Anything they do is watched with interest. We wonder if we can match their talent. If they are complimented, we compare their comments with ours. Even if we have good friendships with them, in the background we are concerned about how we measure up to them. The ego manages to turn service into a competition. How much we are growing internally is not a major concern, but how popular and credible we are is.

Being in competition can sometimes awaken an enthusiasm to serve better. When we see others raising the standard, we know we have to work harder to do the same. Their success makes us realise we can do more, we can find another gear and deliver to a higher level.

But the ego of Shakuni does not stop here. Rather

than using competition to further ourselves, it makes us look at others and hope they do worse. We do not want them to steal our crown. Raising our own bar is not a major priority, but hoping they do not raise theirs is. While we may not do anything to make them fail, where possible we can subtly try and stop them doing as well as they could. We might for instance hang onto opportunities that they might be better at, or we might not offer our help when needed.

Instead of promoting and encouraging them to be the best they can, we hold back and restrain ourselves from being of service to them. Although we do not actively dislike them, we see them as a potential rival that we have to be careful of. When we hear they are doing well there is a degree of envy, and when they are unsuccessful there is a quiet sense of satisfaction. The ego stops us working in a team and seeing the greater good. Throughout all this we may appear to be innocently interested in what is going on around us, but there is a part of us that is working out what we need to do to stay ahead.

Along with this competitive mindset, we become tactical about what kind of service to offer. With Dhritarashtra we were always trying to escape our duty, but with Shakuni we specifically use serving as an opportunity to shine. Whenever we are asked to do something we try and work out how to use it to promote our image. We want to know how many people will be a part of it, and if the right individuals will be there to see us. If possible, we try to negotiate the situation, so we get more of the limelight and more of the credit. If the task is too low key, we are not interested in putting in the effort. If we are offered a big stage, we dive in with full enthusiasm. Instead of acting selflessly, our attention is more on finding out how we can promote ourselves to as many people as possible. In place of striving to go deeper into our path, we want people to sit up and take notice of who we are and what we are doing.

With Duryodhana the ego wanted relationships primarily for pleasure and emotional support, but with Shakuni, it goes further and uses others to specifically boost our profile. This does not mean we do not care about people, or that none of our relationships are genuine. But there is a part of us that is drawn to certain individuals because we see them as higher up the social hierarchy. Either they have a significant position in the organisation, or they are particularly talented, or they are close to the Master. The truth is that without these attributes we would not be giving them the same kind of attention. The prestige that surrounds them attracts the ego. Being in their presence makes us feel like we are part of the elite; somehow, we believe that their status can rub off on us. As a result, we give them more time, we willingly go the extra mile and we put more effort into the friendship. Subtly, there is a hope we might get more respect, and extra liberties or perhaps more access to the Master. .

When we are secure in ourselves, we are indifferent

to the success and failure of others. Everybody is viewed the same and nobody is given preferential treatment. We measure ourselves not on where others are, but on where we should be. It does not matter if somebody is successful  in their service or dear to the Master, what matters is are we? Time and energy are not wasted on working out where we stand amongst our rivals, it is driven towards self-enquiry.

This does not mean we are oblivious to what is going on around us. We see when people are doing well and when they are struggling, but there is little judgement either way. They do not take up our mental space and we do not incessantly try to work out what their situation means for us. We have our path and we have no need to unnecessarily bother ourselves with what goes on outside of it.

Shakuni Plays the Game of Dice for Duryodhana – When the Ego Uses Spiritual Insights and Knowledge to be Noticed

The Pandavas have both righteousness and military might on their side. If the Kauravas are to seize their kingdom, they cannot hope to defeat them in open battle, but through the game of dice they have a way forward.

Duryodhana uses Shakuni to get what he wants without having to face the Pandavas in open war. It is both deceitful and cowardly, but it provides a way of realising his aim. In the same way, the ego is looking for a way to conquer without the risk of sacrifice. It wants the glory of appearing spiritually advanced without the hard work of actually transforming.

By expertly understanding spiritual ideas and insights we can convince ourselves and others that we are an evolved seeker. One that is wise and profound. When we have read enough books, listened to enough talks and attended different workshops, when we know all the profound sound-bytes and eloquent quotes, we have sufficient knowledge to start showcasing it to others. We can utilise ideas to fake an elevated stage of advancement.

The need for attention and recognition means we are keen to prove our worth to as many people as possible. As soon as somebody raises a doubt or a need for clarification, we are the first to jump in and offer our thoughts. Every answer we give is delivered with absolute certainty. The ego makes us provide foolproof explanations for things we do not know for sure. We talk about karma, the will of God, past lives and destiny. We act like we know the cosmic plan. If somebody is facing a problem, we pretend with confidence that we understand what they are going through and have the way out of it. There is no speculation, we are clear and emphatic. Even if we do not have the answers, we always feel the need to offer something and pass it off as fact. The ego stops us confessing our ignorance. We do not want others or even ourselves to recognise that we have gaps in our understanding.

The absolute statements we make are an attempt to be noticed. Subtly we are asking for attention. To others it looks like we have immense knowledge and confidence, we seem self-assured and at ease. But deep down, behind the bravado, we are unsteady. The constant need to express our so-called wisdom only demonstrates our obvious insecurities.

Real confidence is being comfortable in not having all the answers. There is no shame in admitting that our knowledge is limited. The last thing we do is pretend we know something when we do not. Whenever somebody has a question, even if we think we have the answer, we are keen to hear what others have to say. As much as we are ready to share our thoughts, we are ready to learn from other people. Most importantly we understand that insights and wisdom are not trophies to hold up, they are meant to take us further on our path.

But without realising it spiritual ideas can be used as scaffolding for the ego to sit on. The accumulation of insights allows our mind to spin out a whole universe of concepts that have answers for everything. We have ready-made explanations for all aspects of spirituality. Most of them are not grounded in experience, they are theoretical understandings that we have thought about or gathered from other sources. Each time we work out a new idea, we think we are spiritually advancing and moving somewhere.

That 'somewhere' however is just an understanding, an increase in clarity. It can be useful if we are ready to implement it on our path, but this is not our intention. Like Shakuni plays the game of dice to avoid war, the ego uses these insights as a shortcut to appearing spiritual. The will to inwardly transform is set aside and gets replaced by a strong desire to understand everything. Subtly we believe that to know is to conquer. The more we are able to understand, the more we think we are winning.

Superficially we clearly see we have flaws and we understand that real spiritual realisation is still far away. Nevertheless, while holding this obvious truth, the ego simultaneously makes a deeper part of ourselves believe we are almost there. Within us, because we 'know' so much, we think we have unravelled all the mysteries of life. Despite our faults, inside we feel like there is very little left to do. We unconsciously believe self-realisation is round the corner. Because of this, we become less aware of the work we need to do. Our faults are perceived as insignificant in relation to the progress we think we have made.

Whenever we actually do self-analyse, we foolishly feel that simply recognising our weaknesses is the same as transcending them. We assume that by working something out we have risen above it. We are unable to appreciate how deep and how serious our problems are. The ego lures us into feeling we are safe and secure. Other people need to be vigilant of their negativity, but we understand how things work. We know the pitfalls and traps that a spiritual seeker can get lost in. Dangerously, our immense theoretical understandings give rise to a lazy, complacent attitude that makes us overlook what we should be addressing. This is exactly what the ego wants.

Just as Shakuni does not want Duryodhana to go to war and face destruction. The ego does not want us to go within and face our issues. It desires unearned wisdom that we can expertly talk about. Despite all our 'profound' insights, we cannot see the insincerity of cherishing ideas which call for change, without actually changing ourselves.

Fundamentally, if there is no longing for Truth, all spiritual concepts are at best useless or at worst sustenance for the ego. They become commodities that we can pick up and use for our own ends. We expertly say what needs to be said to impress and teach whoever might be listening. So long as we are popular, and the ego is getting what it wants, we are content to keep playing the game.

Cunningness makes us lose integrity. When talking to others we can put forward all kinds of profound points. We know how to dress them so that we can come out looking humble and sincere. For example we often mention how ignorant we are, even though we feel like we know a lot. We publicly declare how untalented we are despite being quite proud of our capabilities. Our statements appear innocent and incredibly wise, but although we can explain them beautifully, we have little appreciation of their depth. The problem is we have the insights of a sage but the psyche of a child. Our words are poetic, passionate and compelling, but are not based on any sincere conviction.

When speech is continuously used to maintain falsehood, then what we say becomes increasingly untrustworthy. Words become meaningless, or worse deceptively wrong. At its peak, we can even end up becoming a pathological liar. Not only do we deceive others, we end up being the victim of our own language. We ourselves get sucked into the false ideas we talk about. Our tongue is faster and more compelling than our heart. Instead of truth being realised and then spoken, we speak first and then later claim it as truth. When knowledge is thrown out in such a cheap way, the gap between what we say and who we are becomes increasingly large.

Shakuni Wins Draupadi in the Game of Dice – When the Cunning Ego Legitimises Temptation

The game of dice reaches its climax when Shakuni finally wins Draupadi. She is dragged into the assembly by her hair. She appeals to her five husbands to be saved, but none of them come to her aid. The Kauravas hurl insults, while Duryodhana strikes his thigh and mockingly calls for her to sit on it. Despite all her protests, the evil Dushasana approaches, grabs her sari and tries to disrobe her in public. The scene demonstrates the consequence of what can happen when the cunning ego remains unchecked.

Just as the Pandavas and the elders hold back Duryodhana's behaviour, our conscience and sense of discrimination keep the ego contained, but the gambling match changes everything. This is where Shakuni really comes into his own. He starts by wagering small. A few items of jewellery are won, then horses, soldiers and a whole kingdom are gambled. Eventually, the Pandavas lose themselves and Draupadi. On paper Shakuni has done nothing wrong. He has apparently played fairly and within the rules. Everyone in the assembly knows that something terrible is happening, but no one has enough of a case to hold Shakuni to account. The cunning ego works in the same way. It tries to get away with as much as possible whilst just staying within the law. Even if we feel that what we are doing is wrong, because we can find a clear line of thought to justify our actions, we carry on. Just like a magician is able to pull objects out of an empty bag, the ego conjures up logical arguments to make our behaviour stay above suspicion.

Without self-analysis and sincere vigilance, little by little we bet away all the virtue we have. Through deviousness and irresponsibility, the ego is gradually allowed to eclipse everything that is good. This process starts within the mind. Just like in the game of dice, the ego has to win little things first; perhaps we entertain a thought that we know is wrong. Then this is allowed to

180

develop into a mild fantasy that we repeatedly think over, not long after, we start to look for situations where we can make this a reality. Like a temptress, the ego is always flirting with our conscience and pushing the boundaries of what is acceptable. Every step is just a little more than the last. Because we are not doing anything that is suddenly and dramatically wrong, it all seems permissible. We have enough rationale to justify why our thoughts and behaviour are acceptable.

Cunningness has the power to make the unjustifiable become justified. The Pandavas have the greatest kingdom and Yudhishthira is the most respected ruler in the land. But after a few throws of the dice, they lose everything. In the same way, in a short space of time, years of spiritual progress can come crashing down. When we desire things we know are not meant for us, when we gradually betray the disciplines and commitments to our path, we risk undermining all that we have achieved. The ego makes us succumb to temptation and start drastically straying from our dharma. We know what we are doing is wrong, it is clear we are venturing down a road which is completely opposed to the principles we hold. But we want what we want. Our mind creates so many cover stories to suppress our conscience. Somehow, we manage to behave in a completely reprehensible way and still believe we are being loyal to our path.

The humiliation of Draupadi, is more than losing spiritual progress, it is where the ego disgraces who we are. Just as she is transformed from a queen into a slave, blessings and sacred opportunities are abused for personal gain. The innocence and humility which kept us pure is replaced with a deep corruption.

Cunningness Allows the Ego to Gain Fame and Influence Over Others

The cunning ego can make us so unconscious and divorced from our path, that we see nothing wrong in using all our knowledge and talent to get as much fame as possible. We want to be a kind of celebrity, where fans look at us with awe and whisper how great we are. We want a profile that demands respect. All the while we tell ourselves we are only doing this to help others. Under the banner of service we are ready to dance and perform for the crowd.

When we are sincere, we guard our spiritual experiences, or at least only share them with people who can appreciate them. They are meant to deepen our connection with the Divine. The ego however, uses them as a means to buy the praise of others. We want everybody to know how advanced we have become. People must see just how dynamic and exciting our realisations are. The ego loves to sensationalise what we have discovered in the hope of gaining attention. That which is sacred is shamefully showcased to gain meaningless approval.

This need to prove ourselves, can also evolve into a desire to control others. Before we were just happy to impress people with our profound explanations. When this instinct evolves, we end up wanting people to come to us for advice; we enjoy playing the role of the wise mentor who can guide others on their path.

The ego loves being the one who sorts out their problems. If we have a position of authority, or if we have some proximity to the Master, we can use this to our advantage. People will see us in a higher regard and trust what we say more. Those who are unsure about where they are on the spiritual path end up gravitating towards our self-assured persona. In a way we become a kind of guru to them. While we may often reference the Master's teachings, we actually want them to see us as the authority in their life.

If we are secure in ourselves, we only give advice out of genuine concern and crucially we always refer everything back to their path. All guidance looks to return the other person to their relationship with the Divine and makes them see how to strengthen it. We do not want them to be dependent on us, we want them to progress and be clearer about what they have to do.

At its extreme, the ego does the opposite. It can make us move from offering frank advice, to insisting people follow the life plan we have set out for them. It wants to hold on and keep others subordinate to us. If our advice is rejected by someone, we hope they face the consequences of ignoring us and if we are proved right, we are quick to step in and tell them how they should have listened to us in the first place. Even when our advice turns out to be wrong, we are like a politician able to do all kinds of mental gymnastics to make out we knew what we were talking about all along. Our aim is not to help or push others higher, we just want to preserve the image of one who is great and wise.

Although it is Duryodhana who humiliates Draupadi, it is Shakuni who provides the means. Similarly, while we may have a desire for pleasure and gratification, it takes the cunningness of the ego to work out a way for this to happen. Its deviousness erodes our principles and makes us feel comfortable straying from our path.

Shakuni Sees Krishna as His Equal – When the Ego Believes It Is on the Same Platform as the Master

In the camp of the Pandavas, Krishna is their councillor and Shakuni occupies the same position with the Kauravas. Despite his immense intelligence he is unable to perceive Krishna's divinity. He knows Krishna is 'special', he knows He is no ordinary human being, but still Shakuni cannot recognise Him as the Supreme Lord. When the Kauravas appear to be gaining the upper hand then naturally he starts to believe he is superior. Deep within us, the ego does the same. No devotee consciously thinks they are above the Master. We all believe He is divine, and our job is to listen and follow His teachings.

The constant disobedience and the inability to sincerely follow His guidance, however, reveals a different truth. While of course, we can all struggle to do everything the Master says, most of us still have a sincere desire to do our best. At the very least we do the simple practical things He asks of us. We keep to the rules, uphold certain disciplines and carry out the service that is required.

But like Shakuni, the ego has little respect for the Master's instructions. Whenever we want something, we find a way to put them to one side so we can pursue our desire. No matter how much we say we trust and hold the Master as the highest authority, there are moments where we believe we know better than Him. This is a particular problem if we have followed Him for many years. After some time, we start to feel that we have seen all there is to Him. We know His teaching, we understand the way He thinks and we know what His response will be to almost any situation. The blind, overconfidence we carry means there is no mystery left to the Master. We have worked Him out, and we believe there is little left to learn.

During these times the ego is particularly good at choosing which part of the Master's instruction we have to follow. Even if there are clear, unequivocal directions not to do something, we find a way of doing it anyway. We believe much of His teachings do not apply to us, they are for new devotees or those who have yet to find their way. Often, we might find quotes and take them out of context, or we use advice given to people who were in totally different situations and apply it to our own. Just as Vidura and Bhishma are aware of Shakuni's intentions, deep down inside, beneath all the reasoning, our conscience knows what the ego is doing.

Perhaps the most dangerous time is when after disobeying the Master, things actually start to go well. Inside we can begin to question if He really knows what He is doing. Superficially we still believe in His Divinity, and we still tell others the same, but underneath, we begin to see Him as fallible. We judge His every move and question why He does what He does. We scratch our heads and count up the errors and mistakes He is apparently making. If we allow this to escalate out of control, we end up reducing Him to an ordinary person. The irony is that we carry all these sentiments while openly serving and declaring Him to be the goal of our life.

When the Pandavas lose everything in the gambling match, it looks like the Kauravas have the final victory. Whatever blessings Yudistira received from Krishna have not borne fruit. Even when Krishna comes to Duryodhana asking for peace, once again he fails. Shakuni does not see that Krishna is playing a much bigger game. There is a cosmic plan in which all the arrogant kings in the land are deliberately being brought to the battlefield. In the same way, we take everything the Master does at face value. When the results of His actions do not meet our expectations, we write them off as mistakes. When what He says does not conform to our logic, we assume He has not understood things properly. We cannot see He is operating on a completely different plane. The ego can only perceive a fraction of what is really going on.

For the Master, the material world is a sideshow to the spiritual reality. But for us this material world is all there is. The problem is that with little knowledge we draw absolute conclusions on everything. The arrogance of the cunning ego makes us completely miss the glory of who the Master is.

Life Lessons Rising Beyond the Hypocrisy of Shakuni

- **Get Rid of Your Game Plan**

The ego of Shakuni is defined by duplicity, in other words it is about always having an ulterior motive. This does not mean we are never sincere, it means that when we want something, we adopt a certain game plan to get it. The key out of this, is to try and be as simple as possible. If we are attracted to something that is wrong, we have to be emphatically honest about it. This will not magically eliminate the desire, but it will remove the deviousness in our behaviour.

The ego will always try and over complicate very straightforward issues. When we are simple, our thinking is clean and brief. Instead of piling different explanations on top of each other to justify what we want, we should go back to first principles. Is what we are doing in line with our path? Are we following exactly what the Master has taught us? Most of the time we can answer these with a simple yes or no. Where things are black and white, the ego will always try and create ambiguity. That way it can create a justifiable path to have its way.

<u>Practical Step</u>: Learn to trust your first instinct. The initial feeling that springs forth in any dilemma is usually the one that is correct. If you wait too long, there is a chance for the ego to decorate and distort it. To combat cunningness, we need to act promptly, before it gains momentum.

- **Learn to Stay in Your Lane**

  This path is about us and realising our purpose; nothing else matters. Whenever our attention is somehow drawn to others, instead of allowing the ego to seize upon it with judgement, we have to use their success and failures as a mirror for what we are doing. The great things people do should be seen as an example that we can aspire for. The mistakes others make have to be taken as warnings for what can happen to us. A key symptom that we are straying out of our lane is the enjoyment we get from watching and talking about other people. If we relish looking over our shoulder at whatever everybody else is doing, then we know we are sowing the seeds of Shakuni.

  <u>Practical Step</u>: As much as possible what you notice about others, should be referred back to yourself. Ask what you can learn from their situations. Do you see new opportunities for development that you thought were impossible for you? And how

close are you to making the same errors as those around you?

- **Understand the Importance of Words**

  Words have power particularly when articulating spiritual truths. Speaking about our path is a profound honour and responsibility. It is a chance to plough the depth of our soul and deliver it to others. It is a form of worship where we can present the sacredness within our hearts. We should be careful about the statements we are making. Just because we are saying all the 'right' things it does not mean it is coming from the right place.

  Reading wise words, does not automatically give us the right to play them off as our own. Speaking about the spiritual path has to come from an inner experiential place. When we are talking about things outside the realm of our experience, we need to make this clear. Things we do not know for sure, should not be passed off as truths that we know for certain. We should be weary of getting carried away with profound insights. This is not as easy as it sounds. It requires us to regulate our speech, not just in a spiritual context, but in every aspect of our life.

  <u>Practical Step</u>: Be aware of everything you say in every situation. When you declare you are going to do something, do it. When you promise to

meet someone, meet them when you say. When you praise somebody, it is important to mean it and not just do it out of politeness. The more you live up to your words, the more they will carry the power of Truth.

- **Learn to Give and Receive Advice**

Being sure about what we think is a great thing. It allows us to speak with clarity and take decisive action. The insights we have and the ability to correctly diagnose problems are a precious gift. They can be used to help people change and work through their issues. But no matter how great we are at doing this, we cannot assume this is an indication of how advanced we have become. Just because we can successfully analyse spiritual problems, it does not mean we have some immunity to them ourselves. We should see to it that the confidence we gain from being right in our thinking does not make us stray into complacency.

When we become too sure of ourselves, we can lose touch with what other people are going through. Even when trying to help them, we can become insensitive to their condition. Before advising anyone, we should take the time to listen and place ourselves in their shoes. If we really want to help someone, we have to stop, be silent and see the world through their eyes, before we offer any answers. Whenever we advise people, we should remember we do not have ultimate solutions that can solve all their issues.

That said, we can make a difference. The advice we give should always inspire others to be stronger and clearer on their path. It should not encourage the other person to be more dependent on us.

Practical Step: Do not assume you fully understand the problems of another person without fully listening and digesting where they are coming from. At the same time make sure that your interactions are productive. Do not encourage the other person to unnecessarily come to you. Where possible help them to be strong and independent.

Just as we might be a useful advisor, we also have to be willing to take advice. This requires a willingness to see another perspective. The ego has to realise that we do not have to be right about everything. The refusal to be vulnerable and ask for help is a symptom of pride. Listening with an open mind can break the attachment of always wanting to be right. When we are humble, we see that knowledge can come from anywhere. Everybody has a life experience that we do not have. Even the seemingly 'least spiritual' person can teach us something, if not through their words, then through their choices, tragedies and successes.

<u>Practical Step</u>: Have some individuals around you, who see the world differently. Consult them and analyse why they may come to different conclusions. You do not always have to agree with them, but take what they have to say seriously. In this way you can avoid being in an echo chamber where your opinions are always supported.

- **Understand the Power of Not Knowing**

Following on from this, there is a deeper reason why we should understand the limitations of what we know. When we assume we have all the solutions then we close the book on spiritual development, there is no room for divine mystery. We have to understand that Divinity is transcendent and therefore beyond the mind. Even though we may have so many ideas and insights, they are only limited approximations to reality, not reality itself.

When we say 'I do not know' we open up the landscape of our spiritual path. We remove the barriers that restrict what spiritual experiences we can and cannot have. Understanding how life works is important, but it needs to be balanced with an openness to the unknown. Then from a place of humility we can invite the Divine to show Himself, not as we think He should be but as He actually is.

Knowledge can ground the mind, but it is the

mystery of the Divine that opens up the awe and yearning within our heart.

<u>Practical Step</u>: Alongside any confidence, it is healthy to carry doubt about your ideas. This is not a doubt that brings instability on your path, but it can keep you on your toes, ready to change perspective if it becomes clear that you have to. The aim is to have spiritual insights that navigate you through life, but at the same time, do not enslave you to them.

Bhishma – The Hypocrisy of Dogmatism

The great grandsire of the Kuru dynasty lay there on his bed of arrows like a fallen lion. The blood-stained wounds had all dried, but they were still visible against his silver plated armour. Despite being on the battlefield, despite the terrible injuries he had suffered, he was still fresh and radiant. Bhishma had been discoursing now for over twenty days. Yudhishthira, the other Pandavas and indeed Lord Krishna Himself had all gathered to hear this great man share his knowledge. He had mastered every aspect of scripture, everything from the duties of a king to how to perform sacrifices. He was an expert on how society should be organised and run. The diet we should

have, the various prayers to the Lord and the different methods of yoga practice were all known by him in the minutest detail. As Yudhishthira was to be the next king and Bhishma was soon to leave his body, this conversation was critical. Unless this knowledge was passed on, it would be lost to humanity forever.

But there was one person who remained uncomfortable the whole time. While her husbands listened with rapt attention, Draupadi marvelled at how somebody who was so knowledgeable, strong, and full of pious self-restraint was able to talk so emphatically on the nature of righteousness. She remembered his face that fateful day when her honour lay in the balance. While Dushasana chased her around the hall, she frantically ran to all corners and cried desperately to the kings who witnessed this heinous act. She remembered falling at Bhishma's feet and pleading with him for intervention. His head was lowered, he couldn't even look her in the eye. She shouted for help but he sat there dumb and distant.

Now this great warrior, this so-called wise personality lay there lecturing her husbands on the conduct of a king. Where were his arrows when she was being dragged into the court by her hair? Where were his rich words when Duryodhana and Karna were hurling insults at her?

Bhishma had taken the most extreme of vows, never to marry and never to sit on the throne. He had sworn to protect and serve the kingdom come what may. For this he was renowned as the embodiment of virtue. What a sacrifice he had made, what loyalty he had displayed. He never deviated, he never doubted. Generations passed but he remained. Enemies had come but he vanquished them all. Bhishma had been a constant source of love and guidance to the Pandavas from the moment they had come to the kingdom. But above all he was a devotee of Krishna. Amongst all the drama that had unfolded he could see the Lord's hand at work. Bhishma was one of the few that recognised Krishna as the Supreme Lord, the original cause of all creation. He could see past His human guise and behold the one who sustains everything.

Bhishma once again recalled in his mind that epic scene when Krishna was about to attack him. Wounded by his arrows and seemingly frustrated at Arjuna's weakness on the battlefield, Krishna picked up the wheel of His chariot and rushed towards him like a lion runs at an elephant. Bhishma abandoned his weapons and welcomed the Lord's attack. He remembered the fire of anger in Krishna's eyes and the dust in His hair as He held the wheel aloft. To die at the hands of Krishna would have been the greatest blessing and were it not for Arjuna's intervention, it would have happened.

Despite all of this, Bhishma was on the side of the

Kauravas. During the war his weapons were being used against the Pandavas. His chariot was not drawn alongside Yudhishthira, it was used to shield Duryodhana. Even though he saw the Lord Himself positioned as the charioteer of Arjuna, he raised his bow in opposition. Bhishma was a man of principles but unfortunately, he had become enslaved by them. He staked his life on rules and codes of conduct. These were meant to guide him towards his duty but he chose the letter over the spirit of the law. He possessed every virtue imaginable yet he could not tear himself away from being governed by so called principles of dharma. It was this one vice in his character that made him fight for the Kauravas. His whole life was dedicated to upholding righteousness, yet curiously, he found himself fighting for unrighteousness.

Bhishma Commands Duryodhana's Army – When the Ego Uses Rules and Order to Conquer

With Duryodhana we see how an insatiable selfish appetite exploits everything on the spiritual path. The ego is willing to transgress any rule and tear down any barrier to get its way. Without any restrictions it creates chaos and enjoys manufacturing its own version of spirituality. Pleasure becomes the measure of what is sacred and worthy. Bhishma however, exists on the other end of the spectrum. He is exemplary in his conduct. He sacrificed the throne and refused to marry just to please his father. He is a master of scriptural knowledge and a formidable warrior.

Whereas Duryodhana is striving for his self-interest, Bhishma only lives to uphold dharma, yet this great and noble man finds himself as the commander of the Kaurava army. He has chosen to wield his bow against Yudhishthira, and more importantly against Krishna. The hypocrisy of Bhishma is not really about Bhishma himself, but about the consequences of his serving Duryodhana. It is what happens when the ego uses piety and obedience as a way to strengthen itself. By clinging to dogmatic principles as a cover, it can go out and gain control.

The spiritual path is a potential minefield. How do we know if we are deviating from Truth? How can we be sure we are not being misled? Because we are journeying to transcendence there is every possibility we can venture off into fantasy and delusion. The mind is incredibly powerful and can conjure up all kinds of justifications to legitimise our selfish desires. The antidote to a 'do as you please' freestyle form of spirituality is to follow tradition, it is to be orthodox, to follow rules and regulations. It means being disciplined and living in accordance with the law. Bhishma by himself is exemplary, but when he serves Duryodhana, we see how principles become enslaved by the ego. Life becomes about how strictly we can conform to what we think is expected of our path.

Because we want to be good, we spend hours on our spiritual practice, we work on projects and serve wherever we can. Whatever we do, we follow the instructions which have been given. If we are part of an organisation, we implement exactly what our superiors have told us. If we are part of a tradition, we practise everything that has been passed down. Like a militant soldier, we are rigid, direct and uncompromising in our actions.

Dedication is an admirable and essential quality. Spiritual progress cannot be made unless we are willing to embrace our path with enthusiasm. An uncompromising intensity towards the goal is both precious and rare. The problem in this case is very specific; our motivation is not based on a desire to grow, nor on a longing to develop our relationship with the Divine, but is founded on the ego's desire to dominate. The excessive dedication to rules can masquerade as devotion but is in fact another way to gain order. The ego uses this trait for security and the satisfaction of being right. Qualities such as discipline and commitment are ordinarily traits to aspire for, but here they feed our arrogance and make us feel overly certain about what we are doing.

In this scenario, the ego is not necessarily interested in winning the praise and respect of other people, nor is it particularly bothered about having authority over others.

Whereas Shakuni is all about using intelligence to gain recognition, Bhishma is all about using religious principles to feel self-righteous. In the privacy of our own world we want to believe we are good, that we are doing everything we are supposed to. The closer we stick to the rules the more worthy we become. There is a subtle enjoyment in correctly carrying out orders and doing things by the book. We want to believe that all the boxes have been ticked and we are ahead of the game. Just as Bhishma commands the Kauravas, through rigid dedication the ego tries to tame the spiritual path so that we can feel safe and at ease.

Religious traditions and organisations are immensely valuable. There are rituals and various practices, all of which provide a grounding structure for the mind to anchor itself. It gives us a lens by which to understand how we fit in the world. There is however a profound danger that we can become excessively attached to them. Having a clear framework to follow should provide a portal to go within, but it should not be superficially addictive.

Bhishma has set aside everything for the sake of what he thinks is dharma. He has become so consumed by it, that in certain situations he makes inexcusable decisions. Draupadi's disgrace in the gambling hall could and should have been avoided. Bhishma remained silent and witnessed the whole tragedy. His obedience to the law and the instructions of the king trumped his own inner conviction. In the same way, blindly following rules leads to extreme behaviour. Not only are we not wise, we can end up being foolish. Nonetheless, we think we are justified since we are following the teachings and commands which have been passed down to us.

The ego makes us use religious philosophy to feed the mind but not the heart. It makes us obsess about implementing doctrines, without understanding the principles behind them and where they are taking us. Consequently, we become a fundamentalist, a literalist that operates only in terms of what we have been told and what we have learnt. Our minds are mechanical and robotic. Rules are rules, and regardless of the situation they must be followed. More than any longing for Truth, we are looking to be correct and proper.

Whereas Duryodhana used Shakuni to try and avoid war, he manipulates Bhishma to aggressively engage in it. Similarly, in this situation the ego does not try to avoid sacrifice, it actively runs after it. We are fired up, ready to face whatever lies ahead. We feel safe and secure carrying out duties and fulfilling our role. We are not scared of working hard or giving things up. If anything, the more we get to work, the more sure we are of being correct. Inside we have various insecurities and we struggle to accept ourselves. As a result, we seek to find this acceptance through doing more.

Renunciation is not something we shy away from; we wear it like a medal. We are so convinced that being austere is being devoted that we subconsciously go out looking for more difficulties and challenges to affirm our spiritual progress. Just as Bhishma gives up the throne and the prospect of marriage, we also take on burdens to convince ourselves we are walking the path in the right way.

The Ego Makes Us Narrow-Minded and Judgemental

The fixation with tradition and our dedication to the organisation we are in can make us judgemental. When we have such clear ideas about what is right, then anything that falls outside of our narrow definition is cast aside as

completely wrong. It is considered useless and heretical. Life is black and white; there is no room for nuance and there are certainly no exceptions.

At some level, we see those who are on other paths as following an inferior way. The ego's commitment to being right and proper turns us into supremacists. We develop an arrogance where we are completely sure we have the highest, most direct way to Truth. With Shakuni, the ego uses spiritual insights to gain attention and praise; with Bhishma, it uses them to prove why we have the right path. While the intentions are different, both egos use knowledge with almost no first-hand experience. Everything that is known has been told to us. Whenever there is a chance, we argue and debate meaningless philosophical points. Using scripture and different authorities we build arguments to show why other people should be following our way. At all times, we believe we are serving; we believe we are helping people and bringing them to the light.

The staunch confidence we carry is not based on any deep spiritual conviction. We have simply read and learnt opinions from others. When we peel back the layers, underneath it all we have little inner foundation for any of our beliefs. Instead of using this knowledge to go inwards and grow, the ego uses it as a weapon to demonstrate why we are right. We cannot see it, but the reason why we are constantly looking to prove our path is because we do not fully believe in it ourselves. The truths we preach have not been registered on a deeper level and so we are not secure in them. To compensate for this, the ego goes out on the offensive. By constantly forcing our doctrine and movement onto others, we are trying to force it on ourselves.

When we are secure in our beliefs, when we truly trust in the path we are walking, then we have no need to make others believe what we believe. We happily offer the knowledge that has transformed our lives. We take great delight in sharing what we have been given but there is no loss to us if people do not accept our way. While it is our duty to spread our tradition and support others, we know that whether they actually listen to us or not is not in our hands. The genuine faith we have in our path automatically means we trust in divine will.

As mentioned, Bhishma himself is pure, but all of his auspicious qualities are used to defend the Kauravas. In the same way, the knowledge we treasure is sacred, but the way we hold it in our mind, the way it makes us feel can easily become rooted in pride. Our mind enjoys the security it gives us. Carrying this knowledge does not soften our heart, it feeds a bullish aggression where other paths are seen as categorically wrong. We end up spending more time judging the movements of people than on focusing on ourselves. The ego makes us ready to expose those who have strayed. We constantly point to the book, to the chapter and verse to prove just how right we are.

This aggression looks like one pointedness. 'It is not a vice', we tell ourselves, but an asset, something that is protecting and ensuring our advancement. Those who are broad-minded and liberal in their stance are seen as weak devotees. They have sold out. They are submitting to the opinions of others and bowing to modern day culture; they have forgotten their roots and betrayed tradition. In many ways we see these individuals as worse than non-devotees who have no path. Religious dogma provides a perfect forum for the ego to take centre stage. Under the cloak of religious dedication, we become oppressive. The more wrong we can show others to be, the more right we think we become.

Because we are doing everything we should be and we have made all the prescribed sacrifices, we feel we have the authority to cast judgement. The ego enjoys holding others to the same standard we are apparently hitting. It does not care about their personal challenges and emotional obstacles; these are just excuses to hide behind. Everyone must conform to what is right, exactly as we have done. We do not see that the ego is using our external 'spiritual success' to distract us from going within. We become consumed with changing others, so we do not have to change ourselves.

Bhishma Knowingly Fights Against Krishna – When Rules and Dogma Make Us Miss the Master

Despite this oppressive attitude, not everything we do is wrong. Although Bhishma is fighting for Duryodhana, he is still a devotee of the Lord. When Krishna comes to slay him, he immediately welcomes it as the greatest opportunity of his life. Even while standing against Him, he does not lose sight of who Krishna is. In the same way even though the ego is motivating much of what we do, we are not without sincerity. Throughout life we have moments or periods where we are genuinely connected. There are times when the presence of the Divine is really with us. Underneath the fundamentalism there is a genuine desire to evolve. Extreme dogmatism, although an obvious flaw, does not completely divorce us from our path.

Unfortunately, these periods can easily be overshadowed by the ego. Strangely it is the intensity of serving that makes us forget who and why we are serving at all. It is difficult for us to see, but our commitment to the rules slowly makes the Divine an insignificant sideshow. We can get so carried away with duties that we do not take the time to notice if we are actually connected to our higher purpose or not. Just as Bhishma's loyalty to Duryodhana makes him fight against Krishna, when the ego takes up the principles of a good devotee, it pushes us further from the Truth.

Externally our whole life is incredibly dedicated. There are few who could match us in commitment. The problem is our spiritual path becomes completely about how well we are conforming to what we ought to do. We become entirely results driven. Success is not defined by how we feel within, it is about how well and how quickly we can get something done. Every time we complete a task, it is another battle won. Each conquest gives us a small thrill. We are on top of our game serving exactly as we should be. We do not see it, but instead of being a humble devotee, we have become a dry member of an organisation. Despite all our activity, we are not increasing our devotion, only our commitment to the establishment we belong to.

The tradition designed to take us to realisation of who we are ends up becoming more important than actually attaining this realisation. We have brought into the brand of the product, but not the product itself. Even though these principles and rules have been made to connect us deeper within, we have somehow used them to stop this happening. Everything that surrounds being spiritual has been taken up, but spirituality itself has been left behind. The truth is that there is a significant part of us which is just doing this for ourselves. The work and the service are all being done primarily for our satisfaction. The desire to grow has been suppressed by the pride we feel at accomplishing our duty. Somehow the ego has made us miss the very point of why we are on this path at all.

The situation is so deceptive because all our actions appear to be correct. Just as Bhishma has chosen his idea of righteousness over Krishna, we have chosen to serve rules over going within. We have forgotten that authority is not Truth, Truth is authority. Our connection with the Divine should be more important than simply carrying out orders.

Bhishma Prevents the Pandavas from Winning – When the Obsession with Rules Stops the Inward Journey

For ten long days Bhishma fights as the commander of the Kaurava army. He does catastrophic damage to the Pandava forces. During this time, Yudhishthira and his brothers become increasingly frustrated. Unless Bhishma is defeated, there can be no progress and certainly no victory. Duryodhana on the other hand, is filled with confidence for as long as Bhishma is still alive, the war can never be lost.

The ego gains tremendous security from a self-righteous attitude. Just as the Pandavas cannot move forward when Bhishma is in command, so too we cannot turn inwards unless our reliance on external ideas is put to one side. When our identity is so fixed on what we do, the possibility of finding out who we are becomes difficult. We are so attached to living up to what we think is a perfect devotee, that we fail to become one. We forget that the spiritual path is fundamentally an inner journey. This is exactly what the ego wants to happen. Its job is to push us outwards; it wants to turn our attention to achieving and does everything to distract us from relying on what we feel within.

It is sometimes easier to hold onto ideas which have been given by tradition than it is to search out our own inner wisdom. Disciplined practice is in many ways simpler than self-analysis. The ego fears the defeat of Bhishma because it opens the doorway to real responsibility and inner work. Rules and philosophy provide a clear road. They are safe and secure. They restrict Truth to clear predictable narratives that fit with what we know in our mind. Theology defines it, philosophy tells us the purpose of life, and rules show us the way. It is all neat and tidy. Looking within on the other hand, opens up a new unfamiliar world. When we define progress by doing, it can be easily measured and we know where we stand. Thinking for ourselves and trusting our feelings is a gamble. How can we know how well we are doing and how much progress we are making?

When we trust our heart, it leaves the door open for grace to enter our lives. It allows us to build confidence in our relationship with the Divine. The more faith we can have in our conviction, the more we see we are guided. This is where our service and spiritual practice come to life. Instead of having a dry mechanical path, we experience a sacred presence.

When we are overly attached to a rule-based system, trusting our feelings can be like walking into a black hole. There is no guidance or roadmap to tell us how we are doing. If we turn to scripture, if we follow orders, then as long we stick to them, we believe we are on solid ground. There is no anxiety about going astray or being deceived. But all of this comes at the expense of genuine spiritual experience. The thing that was meant to keep us safe is actually holding us back. However holy this attachment to tradition looks, it is the ego's attempt to run away from going within.

The Ego's Focus on Rules Stops Us Enjoying Life

Because we do not go within, we can end up becoming cold and insensitive. We no longer smile and laugh. We forget that a relationship with Divinity should evoke joy. When there is a heartfelt connection, we have a deep happiness within because we have been touched by grace. When we serve and perform spiritual practice there is an enthusiasm that makes us embrace life. But the ego robs us of this positivity. Everything we do becomes forced and without creativity. We cannot live for the moment and see where life takes us. We do not know how to relax and accept what has to be. Our life has to be planned in meticulous detail; nothing can be left to chance.

Because we do not trust, the ego turns us into a control freak. If there is an upset in our plans, we start to panic. We become obsessive and compulsive in our behaviour. All eventualities must be accounted for, nothing can be left to chance. Beneath our dogmatic certainty there is a tremendous fear of life and this is what makes us excessively seek control. We lack an inner connection and we do not have faith in ourselves, so we try to make up for it by gaining order externally. Although we may say we are grateful for walking this path, we are constantly tense and hardly anything we do is with our heart.

While the ego can make us judge others, it can also make us judge ourselves. Because we always want to hit the mark and excel, we place immense pressure on ourselves. We carry a constant anxiety of doing something wrong, or of not being good enough. We beat ourselves up when we do not meet the standards we should be. This mindset can even get projected onto the Divine. We do not worship out of any devotion, but out of fear. Although we talk about mercy and Love, inside we see God and the Master as more of a dictator.

Fundamentally we do not trust that we are loved. Rather than striving to experience Divinity, we feel we have to simply survive. Despite hearing so much spiritual teaching, we forget that divine Love is unconditional, that it does not judge in the way we do, it does not analyse the successes and failures of our service like we have been doing.

If we do not go within and trust, we can eventually end up being institutionalised by the tradition or organisation we have joined. We need it, not because we want to evolve, but because we will be completely lost without it. We have defined ourselves so deeply with the position and movement we belong to, that we have no idea who we are outside of it. Life is calling us to live, it is urging us to have faith in ourselves and explore. Dogma can condition the mind, but real experience is found within the heart. At some point we have to rest there. Unfortunately, the ego turns us into a child that refuses to grow up. Fighting against the flow of life, we cling to the safety of our principles and do not answer the grander calling.

Bhishma Delivers Wisdom on the Bed of Arrows – When Religious Tradition Becomes Free of the Ego

On the tenth day of the war, Arjuna encounters Bhishma. Standing behind Shikhandi, he begins to rain

212

countless arrows all over Bhishma's body. Blood begins to pour from his wounds, and eventually this mighty hero collapses from his chariot. A ceasefire is called and all the great warriors from both sides gather to honour him. There Bhishma remains on the battlefield witnessing the terrible atrocities that occur over the ensuing days. Eventually after Duryodhana has been defeated, Krishna instructs Yudhishthira and his brothers to visit Bhishma. As his life draws to a close, he teaches Yudhishthira all manner of subjects. This wise and noble person delivers the most profound of knowledge. All the while the Pandavas listen attentively, and all the while Krishna Himself is present.

The fall of Bhishma is where rules and tradition cease to feed our ego identity. We are no longer held hostage by the excesses of religious and organisational dogma. This defeat does not happen easily. It takes ten long days with many warriors failing in their attempts. Only Shikhandi is able to disarm him. To Bhishma, this warrior is not a man but a woman, so no one should take up arms against 'him'. The gender of Shikhandi is a matter of debate and perspective. This uncertainty is what makes him a social anomaly. He does not fit the mould of mainstream culture. Shikhandi stands for the liberal, even rebellious attitude that is needed to break free from the rigidity of tradition.

When Bhishma fights for Duryodhana, the ego convinces us that we have to stay in line and keep below the radar. Our job is to conform, to blindly follow where everybody else is going. To defeat him we need to dare to be different, and we need the courage to break some rules. We need to shake off the stagnation that has developed, and reshuffle our principles. The ego will make us fearful. It wants us to believe we are on a road to damnation. Therefore, we need a defiant mindset to 'stray' away from the norm. We have to be immune to the judgement of others and be ready to jump out of our normal boundaries. This attitude is essential to moving on from the conditioning we have signed up to. Spirituality is individuality and our goal is not to conform to the expectation of others, but to be ourselves. Spiritual realisation is not achieved as a group; we walk this path alone not as a tribe. At some point therefore, we have to understand how to take our place as an individual.

Shikhandi is not a warrior that can defeat everyone. He is certainly Bhishma's Achilles heel, but he is not able to kill the other commanders of Duryodhana's army. In the same way this rebellious attitude is precisely the solution to free us from the chains of social conditioning and religious fundamentalism, but it cannot be used in other situations. There must be a purpose to deviating from the norm. We have to clearly identify the constrictions that are holding us back, only then does this stance become justified. If the ego gains power through order, then the antidote has to be more chaos. Too much chaos however, inevitably leads to a lack of direction and confusion. A rebellious way of thinking is easy for the ego to use, as it feeds into the Duryodhana mentality. We feel unique and different to everyone else. The fight between Bhishma and Shikhandi is the balance we have to strike between order and chaos.

It is important to note that the defeat of Bhishma is not the death of Bhishma. Once he has collapsed onto his bed of arrows, he is removed from Duryodhana's control and is free to be himself. At the end of the war, Krishna tells Yudhishthira as a matter of urgency to go and learn from this wise man before his knowledge is lost to the world. Similarly, our aim is not to destroy tradition but to eradicate the ego's influence. Once this has been done, philosophy and rules can be used to help us grow on our path. They no longer become the noose around our neck starving us from spiritual nourishment, but an important platform upon which we can grow. They safeguard us against disappearing into vain fantasies. Organisations provide boundaries and a clear vision of what we have to attain. Instead of a prison, they become a wonderful forum through which like-minded individuals can gather and inspire one another.

During the many days of Bhishma discoursing, Yudhishthira receives immense wisdom on how to live and how to worship; all the while Krishna too is present, silently listening. When Bhishma fought for Duryodhana, he was directly opposed to Krishna, but now the Lord is there listening and enjoying his words. If we adopt a fundamentalist attitude, then inevitably we will be fighting against Truth, we will be against the very thing we are seeking to stand for. If we are able to identify the ego and get the balance right, we will not miss the Master. He will be right there listening and enjoying the rich wisdom we are able to draw from our path. The goal is not to kill Bhishma, but to rescue him from the clutches of Duryodhana.

Life Lesson Rising Beyond the Hypocrisy of Bhishma

- **Rules Must Be Supported by Longing**

  No matter how strongly we follow the rules, it is only a longing heart that brings us closer to the Divine. This is what decides if we are simply living a religious lifestyle or whether we are truly walking a path.

  Rules and spiritual activity should always be supported by a desire to go deep. We have to train ourselves to always feel the depth behind what we are doing, instead of dryly carrying things out. As we do this, instead of the prideful satisfaction of being good, we will develop a natural enjoyment that springs from within. We must try to make everything we carry out externally reflect the devotion we have in our hearts.

  <u>Practical Step</u>: Whenever you are about to carry out any kind of service or practice, pause and as sincerely as possible offer it to the Divine. This will sanctify your actions. Appreciate and enjoy the

opportunity you have been given. Make reaching this attitude as important as accomplishing the task you have set out to do.

- **Develop Broad-Mindedness**

When the ego gets locked into tradition, it enjoys the satisfaction of believing it is the gatekeeper to Truth. While it is natural to want to spread our path to as many people as possible, the ego does not want to offer these teachings, it wants to force it upon others. It makes us believe others can only be saved by following our path.

We need to remember that we do not know what somebody's dharma is. It is not our responsibility to call out and intimidate others to turn to what we think is best. Not everyone is ready for serious spirituality. A strong desire to discover the Truth of life is extremely rare and we cannot expect everyone we meet to abandon the world and walk our path. Just because somebody is not part of our tradition and organisation, we cannot write them off. Rather than bully others to see life as we do, we should support and inspire them to reach their potential in whatever that may be.

This does not mean we should be completely passive. Part of walking a path is loving and protecting it. In a world which has so many beliefs, inevitably there will be some which contradict and even attack our own. Whenever it is threatened, we should be ready to take a stand and defend it. If we have truly felt the benefit of these principles, then there should be an instinctive urge to propagate and keep them alive.

But there is a vast difference between this and actively looking for trouble. We should be careful that we do not mistake our distaste for other paths as love for our tradition. The ego has a habit of indulging in criticism simply to make us feel holier than we are. Real maturity is being able to confidently uphold our path without the need to unnecessarily compare or belittle others.

Practical Step: Remember that you do not know why somebody has been born into this world and what they have to achieve. Everyone has a duty to share their path and inspire others. But do not force or dictate to another individual on how they should live their life.

- **Do Not Measure Spiritual Progress by What You Do**

As much as possible we should remember that it is not what we do that ultimately matters, it is who we are.

Anyone who walks a path wants to be the best they can. But if we define this by how much time we spend on our spiritual practice or other service projects, we can often fool ourselves into believing we are advancing when we are not. If there is any measure of spiritual progress, it is how much we trust that our life is guided.

Having this deep trust automatically makes us grow in our inner relationship with the Divine. Life is not looked at with fear, we are not constantly worried about trying to stay in control because we understand that we are in lap of the Divine and things are being meaningfully orchestrated. This acceptance is what allows us to appreciate our path.

While the love we have for our path naturally manifests as perfection in our service, it does not necessarily work the other way round. Just because we do things well it does not necessarily mean we have devotion in our hearts. We must not be lured into externally doing things as a way of making up for the lack of internal connection we feel. Instead we need to have faith and accept ourselves as we are. We do not need to prove ourselves, we just need to savour the opportunity of expressing our relationship with the Divine through the work we do.

Practical Step: Ask yourself if you were forced to stop all your external service, would you still accept yourself and feel that you are loved in the same way? If the answer is no, then there is a need to deepen your inner relationship. More time needs to be spent in prayer and contemplation. Keep enquiring and search for that inner security.

- **Cautiously Learn to Trust Yourself**

There is always a balance to be struck between a healthy fear of straying from the rules and trusting what feels right. There is no easy way to know how far we should go. The ego can work both sides to its advantage: we can either become a narrow minded fundamentalist, or a rebel who breaks all the rules.

In the beginning we should be cautious. Whenever we are confused and unsure it is always better to adhere to what we have learnt to be right. As we mature, the need to trust what we feel becomes more important. Trusting however, does not mean we are automatically free to do as we please, or that we are above the law. It means we should be looking within for guidance.

Rather than constantly referring to external sources, we must be willing to ponder and work out the right way for ourselves. Errors will inevitably be made along the way, but as long as we are sincere in trying to grow, we will be led back to where we should be. At some point we need to give our uniqueness a chance to breathe, and that involves eventually making decisions based on what we feel. This is what transforms us from a member of an organisation to one who has a personal, direct relationship with the Divine.

<u>Practical Step</u>: Start trusting yourself with small things first. Before making any decision analyse your feelings and work out what your heart is telling you. As mentioned, go with your first instinct. See the results of your choice and reflect upon whether you did the right thing or not.

- **Understand the Importance of Tradition**

It is easy to dismiss religious philosophy and ritual as outdated superstition. However, any religious tradition which teaches us to turn inward and also see the unity of humanity needs to be treasured.

Often people like to be spiritual but not subscribe to the constraints of religious teaching. While tradition is not essential, it has the potential to transform our path. Living a disciplined life and understanding it through a certain philosophical lens anchors our devotion. It focuses the mind and provides a base which allows us to go deeper into our path. It also places us in the company of other like-minded individuals, who can support and further inspire us.

While there are always going to be core principles which we cannot compromise on, tradition needs to have a degree of flexibility. It has to be dynamic and relevant to the times we live in. Situations vary and our interpretation of religious teaching should reflect that. This is why it is important to work out why these rules and principles exist. Some may be specific to old ways of living, others may have direct implications for how we view the Truth. It takes time and a depth of understanding to distinguish between the two.

Practical Step: Educate yourself about the philosophy and practices of your tradition. Read scripture and the writings of previous saints. Do not settle for just superficial learning, internalise the wisdom you have learnt. Use this knowledge as the lens through which you see yourself and the path you are walking.

• **See that the Divine is Never Far Away**

The positive side of this ego is that we are never far away from the presence of the Divine. Even if we display arrogance, even if we are shackled by dogma, the fact that we are still serving, means God remains close by. Other kinds of ego can drastically take us away from where we should be, but with Bhishma the desire to do what is right and the determination to work for it are strong. These priceless qualities mean we are not completely divorced from grace. Of course, there needs to be a shift in perspective, but if we can do this, we will immediately place ourselves in the right position. Just as Bhishma never loses his devotion to Krishna, deep within us the desire to spiritually advance is always there, we just need to rediscover it.

<u>Practical Step</u>: There will be moments where you feel deeply connected. Do not ignore or overlook them. Instead of rushing on to the next thing that needs to be done, take time to deepen what you feel. Cherishing such moments is what the spiritual path is all about. It is the reason why we serve at all.

Karna – The Hypocrisy of False Compassion

Krishna had just left, and Karna's head was spinning. In just one short encounter his whole world had collapsed. The greatest of all wars was about to commence. Karna had spent years itching to demonstrate his skill. Finally, he had the right platform where history would judge him, and not Arjuna, as the best of warriors. This was the time to please his dear friend Duryodhana and grant him the victory he so desperately yearned for.

Now Karna had been given the revelation that his arch

enemies were in fact his brothers and Queen Kunti was his mother. He was struggling to come to terms with the implications of this. Here he was about to go to war and slaughter his own flesh and blood. Arjuna was in every way his nemesis. Ever since they first met, a toxic rivalry had been ignited. What was he to do now? Did Krishna really expect him to give up his whole cause and switch sides? It was a request that he could never fulfil.

Karna had given himself to Duryodhana without reservation. When the Kauravas and Pandavas were first displaying their martial talents all those years ago, he remembered his eruption into the arena. He openly challenged Arjuna, to decide once and for all who was really worthy to be named the greatest warrior. Karna was on the cusp of proving himself to the world. When questioned by the elders as to who his parents were, he was left silent and humiliated. It was openly announced that a charioteer's son had no place engaging with a royal prince. Their verdict still stung him today. In that moment when the whole world looked away, Duryodhana stepped in and crowned him king of Anga state. Honour was everything for Karna, and since

Duryodhana had saved his, he owed him his life.

So what if Kunti was his mother? Why should he suddenly give up all his integrity for a woman who abandoned him at birth? Where was she when he was being disgraced? Karna grew increasingly angry as his mind was being ripped apart. He knew only too well that his friendship with Duryodhana was not pure. The Pandavas were formidable on the battlefield and the hundred brothers were no match for them. With Karna fighting on their side they were a force to be reckoned with. This was why Duryodhana seized the opportunity to rescue him. It was a tactical business relationship as much as anything else. You would have to be a fool to not see the obvious vices in Duryodhana; he was intensely selfish and would make a dangerous king.

In contrast, Yudhishthira was an ideal ruler, righteousness was firmly on his side. Everyone knew the kingdom belonged to the Pandavas; they had suffered injustice and insult at the hands of his dear friend. He himself had been influenced and stained by the vile acts of the Kauravas.

Despite realising all of this, Karna could not forsake his loyalty to Duryodhana. He had surrendered to him. Heaven and earth may perish but this bond would not break. Karna's compassionate deeds were known far and wide. He defined himself by his kindness for others. Now fate had arranged this great war where he would be fighting not only against his own brothers but against dharma itself. More than all of this, he would be firing his arrows against the Lord. Despite being surrounded by the most ignorant and arrogant people, he knew about the Divinity of Krishna, and wherever there was Krishna, there was bound to be victory.

Karna was no fool, it was obvious that defeat would be inevitable. This war was a march to certain death.

Karna's Generosity- Understanding Compassion on the Spiritual Path

As the eldest son of Kunti, Karna is a Pandava and so does not belong with the Kauravas. His father is no ordinary mortal but Surya, the Sun God. Just as the Sun never stops giving its light and energy on the world, Karna too is renowned for his generosity. Whether you are his dearest friend, or his worst enemy, he is ready to give whatever you desire. His nobility and selfless sense of sacrifice is unprecedented. Nowhere in the world or in the heavens is there a being as dedicated to charity as him. While the Kauravas are driven by greed, Karna defines honour by never refusing anyone what they want. Within the Kaurava camp, he stands out as a glaring anomaly.

Karna stands for compassion. He is kindness and sympathy. He is the instinct that responds to suffering, that wishes to help and serve those in need. His unswerving loyalty is unmatched, and his phenomenal level of generosity is something we can all learn from. Just like the Pandavas, Karna is partly divine; in the same way compassion is a sacred quality. It is a natural trait of any truly spiritual person.

Spirituality is about seeing the Divine sitting in the hearts of every being. The more we advance, the more we will want to help those around us. History is full of saints who sacrificed themselves for the welfare of others. They lived their entire lives for the upliftment of humanity. Ordinarily, we look at the ego as something that makes us selfish and cold hearted. It can cause us to be insensitive and to turn a blind eye to suffering, but we have to be careful in assuming this. While being spiritual means being compassionate, being compassionate does not necessarily mean we are being spiritual. Kindness is not always a symptom of our devotion. So often we assume being nice is part of being devoted to God, but this may not be true in all situations. It is this misconception that allows the ego an opportunity to take control.

Duryodhana Rescues Karna and Anoints Him as King – When Our Self-Worth Becomes Enslaved by The Ego

When Karna faces humiliation, nobody is willing to come to his aid. He is alone, condemned and disgraced before a jeering crowd. In this moment of crisis Duryodhana plays the hero. He sees this vulnerable warrior and saves him.

Karna's anointing as king is where the ego seizes compassion to wield power. It is where morals are used as a cover, allowing the ego to have its way. There is a certain state that makes us vulnerable to this exploitation.

Whenever we harbour deep insecurities about ourselves, when we are unsure about who we are, then we are open to being used by the ego.

 Just as Karna feels shamed by his status in front of the royal princes, we can also feel inadequate and anxious about how we fit in. We may wonder if we are charismatic enough. Do people enjoy our company or are we a burden to them? Perhaps most of all we doubt whether anyone really loves us. When we are low in confidence, we worry about how other people look at us. Like Karna, we feel like an outcaste, anxious and unqualified.

The lack of love we have for ourselves leaves the gate wide open for the ego to enter. Just as Duryodhana sees an opportunity, the ego too recognises its chance. It uses the quality of compassion as a form of protection. The result is that we develop a desperate need to be liked. In every scenario we want to be seen as the nice, caring person whom everyone can depend on. We work to develop a reputation as being the selfless 'good guy'. This is what creates the sense of self-worth we have been urgently seeking. Whenever there is a chance, we are always at hand to help. If anyone needs our support we are ready to be there. This is what makes us feel valued. Now we do not have to worry about fitting in, we can be that person whom everybody loves, whom everyone acknowledges as being kind and selfless.

The constant need to appear virtuous robs us of the chance to be ourselves because we end up seeking approval from others. Other people's opinions become hugely important to us. When we receive praise and friendship, we feel a sense of relief and comfort. At the same time the slightest criticism can profoundly affect us.

The ego makes us afraid of being disliked and so we run around saying 'yes' to anything asked of us. We end up being a people pleaser. It does not matter what the cost is, we are always willing to oblige. We cannot say 'no', because we are too fearful of being written off as a bad person. And if we are judged as bad, our whole identity as 'good' breaks down. Consequently, we can end up becoming a doormat, someone who is used by others. Whenever anyone is in trouble, or there is an inconvenient task that needs doing, we are the person who steps up. Even if somebody is rude or discourteous, we do not say anything. At all times we are eager to maintain our reputation as the ever ready, ever helpful knight in shining armour.

The ego causes us to think that passiveness is humility. We confuse a lack of courage with tolerance. We tell ourselves that it is better to always avoid confrontation. We remember stories of great personalities and how they withstood persecution. By agreeing to the requests of everybody we believe we are being spiritual. But unfortunately our actions do not come from a selfless heart, but from a lack of confidence. Instead of demonstrating real kindness in a truly loving way, we are being enslaved by the judgement of those around us. Just like Karna does not understand he is of royal blood and the son of Surya, we too do not understand our worth. We devalue ourselves and walk around with a begging bowl looking for other people to legitimise who we are.

The royal title given to Karna is only a distraction from his humiliation, it is not a real solution. Duryodhana's intervention transforms him from a charioteer's son into a king. In theory, at least, he has the right to take on the other warriors, and most of all he is qualified to fight Arjuna. Simply making Karna head of a state however, does not tell him who his parents are. It rescues him from the immediate dishonour, but he still has no idea who he is. In the same way, the ego is not out to provide real answers, but it does give us another way to live. It provides a new identity to act out.

The ego is seductive because it provides an immediate answer to our insecurity. Any inferiority complex or lack of self confidence can be buried away. We can falsely believe we are that caring person who is ever on hand to give love. This is our purpose in the world, the reason why we exist. The ego provides a temporary way of coping with self-doubt. Deep down we are just as unsure about who we are, but now we have a way of dealing with it in front of others. Like Duryodhana, the ego cannot give us Truth, but it can provide a band aid to cover the lack of love we have for ourselves.

When we are free of the ego's influence, we do not waste time searching for validation. Finding strength in our relationship with the Divine gives us the real foundation we have been looking for. Even if people around do not fully accept us, it does not matter because we accept ourselves. So long as we have that, we have all we need.

Karna Pledges His Friendship to Duryodhana – When the Ego Confuses Sympathy with Love

After being saved from disgrace, Karna is overwhelmed. In an instant he promises his undying friendship to Duryodhana and no matter what happens he vows to stand by him. The creation of this bond is where moral ideals get confused with spiritual ones. Acts of kindness are not the same as journeying within and finding out who we truly are. In fact, trying to be kind and sympathetic can end up being the complete opposite of being spiritual, because it encourages us to hold to the standards of people around us ahead of the wisdom we have within. The vision of what we think is good has been borrowed from family, friends and wider culture. It is not necessarily correct in all situations, and living up to it may not be what our path is about.

Good actions are not the right currency for spiritual progress. Real advancement requires authenticity and a strong inner connection with the Divine, not simply acting out moral deeds. We do not see that it is perfectly possible to be incredibly nice whilst being utterly insincere. This is a condition the ego is keen for us to fall into.

Whenever we see someone in distress, we try and be the rescuer that takes them out of despair. We give our time, we listen to their problems, we offer advice and comfort. While there may be a part of us that really cares, if the ego is involved, the line between sympathy and Love gets blurred. Sympathy is an emotional reaction whereas Love is completely different. It is not an emotion, but a divine connection based on Truth. It pours forth from who we are as the soul. Real Love knows precisely how to deal with a situation. It knows when sympathy is needed and when strict detachment is called for. It sees a person and knows the right way to take them beyond their difficulties. Love is not some grand form of pity. In fact, if we are acting purely out of pity then we cannot be acting out of Love.

Having said that, genuine sympathy which is not manipulated by the ego is an important quality to have. It allows us to connect with the condition of others. We are made to recognise their pain and we strive to alleviate it. Sympathy is a quality that can transform lives and change hearts. It pushes us to do our utmost to uplift others in whatever way we can.

But this is not how the ego wants to use sympathy; it distorts and pollutes it. There is no selflessness. Instead, our own issues are passed onto the other person. The people we help are made into external representations of our own difficulties. The pity we feel for them is the projected pity we feel for ourselves. Service is not done to support the other person but is used as an excuse to comfort ourselves. The ego does not make us see their pain as ours; but our pain as theirs. The desire to help them then becomes the desire to nurse the hurt and insecurity we have inside. By feeling sorry for them we get to feel sorry for ourselves.

When the ego hides behind sympathy, our actions become based on emotion rather than principles. Principles are foundational truths upon which we build our whole perspective. For instance, having a principle of 'help others to help themselves' shapes how we act. It can prevent us excessively serving others and causing more harm than good in the long run. It provides a flag post to guide how we should respond to those in need. This is what brings clarity and makes our actions consistent.

Emotions such as sympathy are not bad, but they need to be implemented within a framework of principles. Without a proper understanding of who we are and where we are going, following emotions can make our actions incoherent and illogical. They are like the wind and cannot be relied upon. One minute we may be dedicated to our path and walking a certain direction, the next we may gravitate to other movements where our goals are completely different. When we are on a spiritual path, we should view such feelings with suspicion. At times emotions can deliver an intuitively right response, but they can also completely misguide us.

Having clear principles stops us being lured away by too much sympathy. We know where we stand. When we see someone drowning in their problems, we offer them a stick to pull them out; but we do not jump in and drown ourselves in the process.

Karna Rejects Krishna for Duryodhana – When Helping Others Becomes More Important than the Spiritual Path

When the Kauravas and Pandavas are on the brink of war, Krishna attempts a last effort for peace. After failing to convince Duryodhana, He speaks to Karna and finally reveals to him who he is. He tells him that his mother is Queen Kunti and the Pandavas are his brothers. Krishna urges him to come back to where he truly belongs and take his rightful place with Yudhishthira. Despite this shocking revelation, Karna is unmoved and will not leave behind his dear friend. He fully understands he is on the wrong side and is sure to face defeat, he hears everything Krishna has said, but yet his unflinching loyalty remains intact. Karna has given his hand, and nothing can move him. His commitment to friendship is so strong, he is ready to throw his life away for the welfare of Duryodhana.

Such loyalty is usually worthy of praise, but when our ideas of righteousness run in conflict with the Master's advice, our nobility turns into foolishness.

At different stages on our path we will be required to let go and embrace a new phase of life. This may mean detaching from relationships. It may even mean letting go of certain moral codes that we have lived by. All aspects of life must be viewed as a stepping stone, a means to delving deeper within. This is what walking a spiritual path is about. Only God has absolute value. When this is understood, as we develop, we will naturally understand why we have to renounce different things.

Without this clarity, inevitably there will be confusion and resistance. Karna has chosen friendship over following Krishna. He has placed his bond with Duryodhana above the instruction of God. This is where our attachment to the ego becomes so strong that we are unable to follow our true dharma. The narrative of being 'good' has become more than just a way of shielding us from insecurity. We have become so conditioned by it, that we cannot imagine ourselves without it. Even when the Master comes directly and reveals our path, we do not want to follow. We see that He has come to uplift and take us to a new stage of development. We know where we ultimately belong, but yet we have mistakenly fallen in love with a false version of who we are, and we will not give it up.

For the most part, morality and Truth can walk side by side, but as stated morality is not Truth. Having the Divine as the aim is not the same as having virtue as the aim. In the beginning we mistakenly believed the two were identical. The revelation that Krishna brings is significant and makes it clear that they are very different. The Pandavas surrender to Krishna's every instruction and this should have been Karna's path. He has instead given himself to Duryodhana. The devotion that we should have had towards the Master, has been handed over to the ego and no amount of persuasion will change us. The ego tells us it is better to be noble than focused on our path. We turn our back on the Master's guidance and say no to a life which is calling us to rise.

With Dhritarashtra there is a constant attempt to dodge responsibility, we make up or hide behind specific excuses to avoid taking the necessary steps. With Karna, it is not a fear of commitment, it is the belief that helping or being loyal to others is more important than finding the Divine within. We feel that our relationships with friends, family and humanity at large is a higher priority than fulfilling our purpose. The spiritual path does not require us to sever our connections with others, it does not demand that we renounce everything and run to a cave. But it will inevitably influence how we prioritise our life.

When compassion is aligned with the ego, even though we know we have to grow, even if we see that the Divine is waiting for us, we deliberately choose not to take action. Our true potential is denied because of sympathy for others. In our minds we think that they are dependent on us and so we feel obliged to sacrifice our own development for their sake. From one side it looks like a strong and noble stance, but from a spiritual perspective, it is both weak and neglectful. Our decisions are not based on fulfilling the role that has been given to us, but are founded in an inability to shake off the emotional ties which are holding us back.

In order to justify this, we tell ourselves that being nice is always the right choice. We put forward all kinds of arguments: We have to stick by people no matter what happens; the goal of life is not about reaching some Divine state, it is about being there for your neighbour. What is the point in getting self-realisation if we desert the person next to us? Dharma is not about retiring to the forest and giving up on the world, it is about lifting people up out of suffering. Real wisdom, we believe, will make us serve those in need. The arguments are not only reasonable but inspiring. They stir our emotions and give us a heroic sense of purpose.

When Truth is the goal, right becomes whatever deepens our relationship with the Divine, and wrong is whatever takes us away. The situation is crystal clear. In the beginning we are happy to accept this foundational belief, because we believe Truth is good in the way we define it. We think divine Love is like our love and spirituality is about being happy in the way we want to be happy. Truth however, is eternal and transcendent while we are limited and material. Divine Love is not the same as our love, realisation of who we are, does not equate to being happy in the world. The ego has stunted our vision and constricted our aspirations. We want Truth to play our game and use our standards and perspective; but no matter how sure we are of what is moral, if it is not in line with Divine will, it has to be wrong.

The Ego Makes Us Proud of Our Service to Others

Krishna is offering Karna the chance to reclaim his true position. This great and powerful warrior is wasting his life with Duryodhana, and at least now, when the war is about to begin, he still has a chance to rise up to his status and stand with the Pandavas. When we choose to be moral, we believe we are acting out of love, but the Master wants to show us what real Love is. He does not want us to continue acting out our vision of saintliness, He wants to make us actual saints. This means abandoning all ideas and philosophies. It means dropping all baggage and becoming an empty vessel for grace. If we are really serious about helping people, then fulfilling our highest calling is the way to do it. The Master is out to do just that, He does not want us to settle for anything less. He wants us to rise and offer real Love to people, not our limited version of it.

In the name of helping others, we can often go around giving our time and talent. We may organise big social enterprises and take up grand ventures to help the destitute. Ordinarily, this is a magnificent thing to do. Through our efforts we can help those in need, we can transform lives and make a real difference. But alongside our genuine concern for others, the ego has the potential to use this situation to its advantage. Because it looks so commendable, we can easily develop pride. The image of being a model citizen and a wonderful humanitarian is very attractive. Everything we do is justifiable because the results are impressive.

It is important to mention that organising and carrying out service projects is not at odds with spirituality. When we are sincere in our intentions, there is a harmonious relationship with our path. As we perform our duty, and engage in various activities, we can be propelled deeper within. The Divinity we are seeking becomes visible in the people we are helping. Alleviating the suffering of others becomes a profound spiritual practice. It expands our vision and makes us less self-centred. We learn from the trials of others, we are humbled and see that in the grand picture we are insignificant.

In any attempt to serve there is almost certainly going to be some element of our ego at play. If we wait until we have transcended all negativity, then we will never venture out to do anything of value. We cannot be paralysed by the fear of not being pure enough. But at the same time we should take care that our intentions are not dominated by the ego. When this happens, we do not aspire to be selfless but enjoy the idea of being selfless.

When we are truly serving, we have no interest in savouring and remembering what we have done. As soon as we offer help, we immediately forget about it. It becomes a distant memory, almost as if it had not been done at all. There is no replaying or broadcasting of what we have achieved. We see whatever has been done as simply meeting the need of the situation. But so long as Karna continues to pledge his friendship to Duryodhana, the ego makes us focus on the dramatic difference we make to people's lives.

Behind the refusal to follow the Master is a belief that we are better. The ego tells us that the spiritual fanatics are out for their own selfish bliss, but we are here for the suffering and downtrodden. Inside we arrogantly think we have chosen a superior road. Krishna's invitation to Karna is an opportunity to leave behind this immature mindset, to throw out a life devoted to ethics for a soul relationship with the Divine. It is when the Master tries to expand our horizons for something far more than simply doing good works.

Ethics have their place in society, but it cannot be compared to spiritual realisation. They exist in two different paradigms. We cannot understand what we are turning down. Karna tells Krishna that he knows Duryodhana is wrong and that he also knows he is sure to lose in this upcoming war, but still he cannot forsake his friend. Superficially, we comprehend what the Master is asking us to do. We know the theory and the consequences, but the pride of being good has made us foolish. Loyalty for loyalty's sake becomes our truth. Even if we do not progress, even if we are denied grace and do not achieve our spiritual goal, because we have not wavered in our moral character, we think we have been successful.

Under the banner of virtue, the bond between Duryodhana and Karna makes us willingly cast aside the opportunity to know God.

Karna Becomes Commander for Duryodhana – When Misplaced Compassion Makes Us Fight for Social Justice Instead of Walking the Spiritual Path

After Bhishma and Drona are defeated, it is the turn of Karna to step up and lead the Kaurava army. This is the chance he has been waiting for. Up until now he has had to stand by while Duryodhana and Shakuni have tried to cheat the Pandavas. Now he finally has the stage to show his skill and most of all he has the chance to defeat Arjuna. The appointment of Karna as commander is where the attachment to moral principles escalates to a whole different level. Simply being a moral person is not good enough. We need to do more than perform acts of kindness, we must step out and transform society. Our role is to fight the injustices of the world. Wherever there is exploitation we need to step forward on the offensive. Just like Karna is ready to do battle and fight for Duryodhana, compassion is used to fight for the ego. Under the cover of spreading love to all, we ignore our spiritual calling and embark on an effort to change humanity.

Once again this sounds like a wonderful thing. There is no doubt that trying to uplift society is a good thing to aspire to. Principles such as nonviolence and respect for all living beings should be propagated to the world at large. If we genuinely believe in something, then we cannot be afraid to share it. Unfortunately, when Karna fights for Duryodhana, our desire to make a difference is not because we want to be an instrument of Divine grace, but because the ego wants to feel empowered.

The causes we fight for may well be the same causes that our Master and tradition stand for, but because of the ego, we do not fight for them in a spirit of service. The philosophy of Love which is so central to the teachings of the Master, is taken up and used as a tool to fuel our personal vision of what the world should look like. Instead of trying to live out our purpose and live in accordance with divine will, we get distracted and become a warrior committed to our vision of social justice. Using our personal take on what the Master's teachings are about, we look to fulfil our fantasy of how things should be.

When we develop wisdom, we understand that despite the terrible suffering that exists, the world is a wonderful place, because it is a direct expression of the Divine. When we are connected in our hearts, we see it in every aspect of life. We acknowledge there are problems, but fundamentally the world is good. In contrast, the ego gives us a different lens. To justify changing the world, we need to see as much negativity as possible. Instead of beauty, we perceive suffering and exploitation. Instead of acts of kindness, we see oppressors taking advantage of innocent people. The reason why we so readily dismiss the wonderful things around us is because the ego does not want us to see them.

Rather than accept reality as it is, it deliberately interprets everything in a negative way. It thrives on seeing the world as a terrible place and paints everything in simplistic terms. There are tyrants and victims, there are the rich and the poor, the powerful and the powerless. We do not want to appreciate that the problems of the world are complicated and there are many factors involved. The more black and white things are made to look, the less we need to think and the more we can justify an emotional reaction.

The ego makes the narrative we have in our minds more important than what is actually happening. If the facts do not match what we wish to see, we dismiss them. We have invested so heavily in a specific story that we almost do not care if it is true or not. Even if people end up being worse off because of what we believe, we do not want to see it. Sustaining our idealistic feelings becomes the priority. The ego needs to keep the problems of the world alive, that way we can organise protests, we can start marches and become a real social activist. We tell ourselves we are representing our dharma, we think we are carrying out a divine mission, but the reality is we have become obsessed with our own personal project.

The reason why this is so convincing is because the objections we have with the world are not unfounded. There is suffering, and lots of it. There are oppressors who prey on the weak and vulnerable. There is horrific cruelty to animals. People die and live in misery. It is perfectly justifiable, if not mandatory to raise the alarm on these issues. Social justice does not run against spiritual development. When we are connected with the Divine, we naturally want to see that same light arise everywhere. Wherever the dignity and rights of people are compromised we should do whatever is in our capacity to stop it.

The problem is, the ego distorts these issues to fit our own agenda. It deliberately makes us get carried away with them so that they end up being more important than our spiritual progress. By serving these great causes we drift further away from our path. We forget that our primary purpose is to go within. We are not activists who have to save the world, but seekers who are striving to know the Truth. Although the two are not necessarily mutually exclusive, the ego makes them so. It stops us sincerely and selflessly dedicating our actions to God. Satisfying our emotions is what matters most. Consequently social and political campaigns end up becoming obstacles on our path.

Somewhere in our minds we believe there is a need to usher in a new utopian society where everybody is happy and there is no suffering. The ego gives us an ungrounded and unrealistic vision of the future we should bring in. The truth is that any dramatic shift in the world can only come through spiritual transformation. Only when individuals at large are ready to transcend their own negativity can humanity move forward.

We may not see it, but often the excessive enthusiasm to correct the world can actually be the ego's attempt to compensate for the issues we feel within. Subconsciously, we believe that the more we can perfect the outside, the more we can make up for the lack of perfection in ourselves. The effort to transform everything externally is used as a distraction to looking within. Just like Karna buries the truth of his birth and fights for Duryodhana, we too ignore the problems within and fight for our idea of justice.

Instead of marrying the welfare of the world with realising the Divine, the ego wants us to place external change in society over our own inner development. That way we do not have to contend with the insecurities we have inside. We do not have to pause and work out what our real purpose is and whether we are truly living up to it. Strangely, we do not see the obvious insincerity in calling for the world to change, when we ourselves refuse to do so. We have tremendous enthusiasm to transform society, but almost no motivation to change ourselves.

We are desperate to alleviate the suffering of humanity, but we do not want to take the time to fix and enrich the relationships around us. When we are dedicated to spiritual progress, the ungrounded fantasy of being part of some mini revolution has to be abandoned.

Karna is Killed by Arjuna – When False Compassion Is Finally Removed

On the seventeenth day of the battle an epic duel ensues between Karna and Arjuna. They both fight furiously, each releasing various celestial weapons, but no one is able to conquer the other. Then suddenly Karna's chariot wheel sinks into the ground. Placing his bow to one side, he jumps down and tries with all his might to free it. Arjuna observes the rules of war and patiently waits for him, but Krishna intervenes. He reminds him of when Karna insulted Draupadi, but most of all when the Kaurava army outnumbered and slaughtered his son Abhimanyu. He tells him that rules cannot be followed when such atrocities have already happened. Goaded by Krishna's words, Arjuna picks up his bow. He sees the desperate, unarmed Karna trying to move his chariot, but he follows Krishna's instruction. Without any mercy, he releases his arrow and severs his head.

The actions of Arjuna can be judged as cruel and unrighteous. How could he violate the codes of war? What kind of honour is there in slaughtering an unarmed warrior? And most of all where is the compassion in such an act?

The answer is there is not any, at least not in the way we have grown to understand it. Krishna shows Arjuna that to kill Karna, there is a certain ruthlessness that is needed. There is a time for kindness and patience, but this is not it. When our moral narrative has become so destructive and so subservient to the ego, a radical approach is called for. We have to find from within ourselves a sharp principled mindset that will cut through the emotional smoke screen that has developed. We cannot allow ourselves to be sucked in by this toxic sympathy. We have to break free of pity and understand what our life is really about.

In this scene it is not Duryodhana advising Arjuna, it is Krishna. Similarly, this approach is sanctioned by the Master and not the ego. He is the one who gives the instruction to kill compassion. He can see when uncompromising detachment from the situation is warranted. If we take this stance under the influence of the ego, then all that will happen is the cover of compassion will be abandoned and we will become openly hateful. We will become cruel and cold hearted. There will be no deceit or duplicity, just a blatant disregard for human welfare.

Krishna's words to Arjuna are a call to come back to the path. The pursuit of a moral campaign has led us so far away from Truth that only an unflinchingly brutal attack on the situation can restore order. The death of Karna is the end of glorifying morality over the Divine. It is where the ego loses one of its closest and most powerful allies. This is when we gain perspective and come back to realising our dharma. It is where we finally understand that the inward journey is more important than any moral crusade.

Life Lesson Rising Beyond the Hypocrisy of Karna

- **Learn to Stop Living for Others**

  It is not easy to work through insecurities. Many of them have developed from childhood experiences. The first thing is to analyse if we are helping people because we genuinely care about their situation or if we are worried about what they will think of us. Do we say yes to everything even when we disagree? Are we constantly giving praise to others because we fear being disliked?

  Any insecurity has to be eliminated by finding security within. We carry a divine presence; the more we live from that, the less we will seek approval from others. We must remind ourselves that if we are on a spiritual path, we are not ordinary people. We live a life governed by grace, and we have a responsibility to honour that. This means we should not demean ourselves for the sake of others. We have a duty to be polite and obliging, but not to compromise who we are. We have to honour our higher calling. As a result we cannot allow ourselves to be used and manipulated. If we live to satisfy the expectations of others, then we are not living a life that is worthy of our dharma.

<u>Practical Step</u>: Treat every person you meet and most of all yourself, as an expression of the Divine. Ignore the judgements of others and remember your position as a spiritual seeker. Do not betray it, by pandering to the opinions of others.

- **Discover Your Path and Stick to It**

Krishna states in the Bhagavad Gita that it is better to do one's own dharma imperfectly than take on the dharma of another perfectly. In other words, our soul has incarnated for a purpose; there is something specific and unique for us to attain.

The challenge of life is to find this purpose and adhere to it at all times. Dharma means living the highest potential we can and not simply following a path we like. The desire to help and change the world is a wonderful thing. Launching humanitarian projects and other activities is certainly a dharma for some, but this does not necessarily mean it is for everyone. Before we invest deeply into something, we have to weigh up whether this is really part of our path. If it is, then we should view these activities as a spiritual practice that strengthens our relationship with the Divine. It must be used to take us deeper within. We should also remember that throughout life, our duty can change. It takes introspection and awareness to discover the right course of action.

Living our dharma has nothing to do with what we want, or what satisfies our emotions. It comes from a deeper intuitive connection. To find this voice there has to be a willingness to pursue any road even if it does not satisfy our expectations.

When we see so much suffering in the world, we can easily feel overwhelmed by it. We may wonder how we can really help humanity. From a spiritual perspective, living out our personal dharma is actually the best service we can do for everyone. By sincerely walking our path we are in fact serving the cosmos at large. We are in alignment with what life wants for us and this in turn benefits all of creation. In short, the best way to help the world's problems is to find and fulfil our purpose.

<u>Practical Step</u>: Finding your dharma starts by accepting that the thing you are doing right now is part of your divine purpose. Embrace this as best as you can, then watch for what life presents to you. Beware of your fantasies and instead trust the flow of circumstances and events that are nudging you forward.

- **Love Is Not Kindness**

Words can be deceptive, and Love is often confused with kindness. Kindness is an instinctive emotional expression. It has immense value. Societies and communities could not survive without it, but this does not change the fact it is limited. Because it is an emotion, it serves the needs of the moment, but not the journey of the soul. Love is different. It is divine and transcendent, it makes the smallest of acts have supreme value. It delivers perfection and gives precisely what is needed.

Whatever is done with Love, however insignificant, is good for us and all creation. As spiritual seekers we are attempting to embody this Love purely. Compassion is something we should always have, but only alongside our connection to the Divine. Beware of excessive kindness, it can sometimes do more harm than good. It can indulge the other person and unnecessarily drag us into the issues of others. Real Love has wisdom. It deals with the suffering of others and causes them to rise.

The more we align with our path, the more we will understand how far to go. Spirituality is about bringing this divine Love to people, not just our sympathy. If we can do that, then we can really make a difference to the world.

Practical Step: Help people wherever you possibly can and try to alleviate the suffering of others. At the same time, understand that until you have realised your relationship with the Divine, there is a limit to what can be done. This understanding brings humility and will show why your inner connection with the Divine is so important. That connection is what can really change lives.

- **Make Personal Responsibility a Priority**

Unless we understand the negativity within, we can easily project it onto the world. If we want to offer proper service, we have to first be proper servants. This involves identifying the ego and understanding how it is working inside us. This does not mean it has to be totally eliminated before we help others, but it does mean we should not be controlled by it.

Personal responsibility is about identifying negative qualities in ourselves first, before launching big ventures to help others. When we are sincere with life, we will have a natural instinct to set our own house in order before we try to change the world. Self-enquiry and honest analysis acknowledges our shortcomings and holds them in check. It stops them clouding our judgement and corrupting our intentions. That way, whenever help is required, we will be more able to give what is really needed.

Whatever we receive from our path is ultimately not for ourselves, it is for the world. This is why focusing on inner development is in itself a form of service. We are making it possible for us to be instruments of Love. We are taking the opportunity to act out our role in a divine plan.

<u>Practical Step:</u> Alongside trying to deal with other people's problems, look for inconsistencies in yourself. Analyse if you have done all you can to nurture the relationships around you. Are you adequately carrying out your duties? Are you aware of your insecurities and fears? If so, what are you doing to move past them? Be mindful of the issues raised by these questions when you help others.

Draupadi – When Helplessness Takes Us Out of Hypocrisy

The screaming could be heard by everyone in the hall. Duryodhana stood up in anticipation, eyes wide and ready to drink in the scene. Yudhishthira refused to look up, he kept staring at the dice which had just been rolled. Everyone in the gambling hall braced themselves for what was about to happen. Suddenly Dushasana entered, grunting and shouting obscenities. The assembly wailed in horror as they saw his hand violently dragging Draupadi by the hair. She frantically cried every time Dushasana pulled her along the floor. Her

lip was dripping with blood and she was dressed in a simple one-piece sari having been ripped from her chambers without warning. Eventually after some struggle she was tossed into the middle of the hall. All eyes were on her yet no one moved.

She scanned the room. There was a deathly silence. She saw her five mighty husbands, without their silks and crowns. She saw the Kuru elders, Bhishma, Drona, Kripa, Vidura all seated. On the throne there was Dhritarashtra with his queen Gandhari. Nobody, not one of them made eye contact with her. She couldn't understand it, for these were some of the greatest warriors that had walked the Earth. They were renowned for their righteous character, yet nobody even lifted a finger. Draupadi cried pitifully, she was barely able to talk. One by one she tried desperately to approach the elders around her. They all sat still, shamefully paralysed by their so-called duty. It slowly dawned on her that dharma had left this place and she was alone.

A shrill peal of laughter broke the silence. Draupadi swung round to see Duryodhana, Shakuni and Karna all staring at her. Like a baby deer caught amongst wolves she waited in terror.

The Kauravas began hurling sordid insults at the once queen. "A woman like her has no honour, we should have brought her in naked!" laughed Karna. Immediately, the Pandava brothers impulsively sprung up to fight, but Yudhishthira restrained and ordered them to hold back. Seeing their provocation, Duryodhana smiled, "Maybe you are right, Karna." He lustfully gazed at her up and down. "Dushasana! I want to see our slave in all her beauty. Remove her sari!" Bhima, Arjuna, Nakula and Sahadeva roared in anguish. They beat the ground and cried, while Yudhishthira looked on like a corpse. The Kauravas cheered and chanted as Dushasana advanced towards Draupadi. She ran across the hall in a blind panic. The shouts grew louder as they watched the chase. Surely now she thought someone would step up and end this abomination, but nobody budged. Suddenly she felt a pull on her sari. Dushasana had caught her, but she desperately grabbed it and reached to get it back. He pulled harder and forced her to the floor. Still trying with all her strength to cling on as she was thrown around, she could feel her whole garment loosening. She cried, shouted and begged him to stop. There was nothing she could do, there was no way out.

Then from nowhere she had an awakening. There was a shift inside, and an inner peace filled her mind. "Govinda," it whispered. The name became louder and clearer, until eventually it overwhelmed and filled her entire being. Draupadi let go of her sari, lifted her hands to the heavens and stood with eyes closed in prayer. There was nothing else but the name and the form of the Supreme Lord Krishna. The people, the assembly hall, indeed the whole world disappeared, there was only Him. Bathed in His mercy and Love, she remained in a state of bliss. Dushasana pulled and pulled, but on and on the cloth kept coming. Finally, Draupadi stood rooted as endless yards of sari of all kinds of colours began forming.

Gradually the taunts and shouts of the Kauravas fell quiet.
The whole crowd was shocked at what they were seeing. It was
Duryodhana now who was in a state of panic. Dushasana
collapsed in exhaustion. The Pandavas, the Kauravas and all
the elders stood motionless; they did not know what to make
of it, they had no idea of the consequences of what they had
done, but they knew they had witnessed the grace of God.

Understanding the Power of the Ego Makes Us Seek Divine Grace

It can seem almost impossible to escape hypocrisy. The ego has the potential to exploit just about any mindset. We can plough ahead with the right reasoning, we can self-analyse in every way, we can be vigilant to the different guises the ego adorns, yet there is every chance we may still fail to recognise the hypocrisy brewing within. By being overly disciplined we can drift into Bhishma's fundamentalism. When we try not to take things too seriously, we can end up dodging our responsibility like Dhritarashtra. How can we be sure we are not suppressing desires like Gandhari? How do we know we are not like Shakuni, cunningly talking ourselves into a fantasy or that we are like Karna confusing sympathy with Love? It seems that in whatever direction we go the ego is waiting to pin us down. With so many potential pitfalls, how can we really trust our thoughts and intentions?

The concerns are real and relevant. Understanding the different types of hypocrisy is important because it gives us a foundational insight into the nature of the ego. It provides a framework to measure ourselves against. Nevertheless, so long as we are still walking a path with an unconquered mind, we are vulnerable. While we can certainly do what we can to hold the ego in check, we cannot eliminate it. Does that mean the situation is hopeless? Strangely, the answer is an emphatic yes.

Understanding that we are completely fallen and a potential victim to our ego, is a profound truth. It takes us down to ground zero. It makes us bow our heads and look to something higher. It returns us to a pure state, where we know nothing. We cannot take pride in our achievements and we cannot be sure we have made any real progress. It sounds negative and depressing, but within this realisation, the Divine is closer to us than ever before. We are left empty and open for something higher to enter our lives. Finally, we see we cannot do this by ourselves. We need help – we need grace.

Draupadi Loses Faith in the Assembly – When We See that the Material World Cannot Give Us Happiness

Draupadi stands all alone in the gambling hall faced with unimaginable dishonour. She is a queen with five warrior husbands, the most distinguished and righteous of personalities are present, but none of them come to her rescue. Helplessness is realising we are caught in the play of this material world and no matter what we have in our life, none of it can grant what we are searching for. It is the understanding that material possessions and relationships cannot give us happiness. Even if we are surrounded by people who love and serve us, even if we have the perfect job or career none of it can deliver the solution we need. We can go through various spiritual experiences, have ecstatic states and many joyous moments, but ultimately even these will pass.

As quickly as things have come, things can leave us. If we are wise, we do not need life to constantly beat us with this truth; we see it, it is undeniable. But perhaps more than this, there is the most obvious of truths: that this body itself will perish. How then can we rely on life in this world? What is the point in investing in a place which is temporary and untrustworthy? Such strong convictions naturally disentangle us from the delusion of material existence. Helplessness is seeing that we are utterly dependent on something higher, it is where we realise we have no other refuge. This deep realisation opens the door to transcendence and allows grace to enter.

Everybody has moments or periods when they feel helpless. When a crisis strikes, we have no choice but to sit back and pray that things turn out the right way. The situation is totally out of our control and no amount of strategising can change the outcome. These situations however, are passing clouds. Eventually the dust settles and normality resumes. We pick up where we left off and go on trying to control things as best we can. As the mundaneness of life takes over, we readily forget how we felt. That feeling of helplessness was just a brief break from the feeling of empowerment.

Real helplessness is not a transient phase that comes and goes. It does not appear when things go wrong and then vanish when they are back on track. It is the foundational position upon which everything else is built. In all circumstances it remains constant. Even if life is showering us with success, even if everything we touch turns to gold, the true state of helplessness does not disappear. Just as a screen is untouched by the movie playing on it, whether we are laughing or crying, celebrating or bemoaning loss, none of it touches the conviction that we are completely dependent on the Divine. For a true devotee, helplessness is the unchanging background of every situation.

The Path to Helplessness

Draupadi's appeal to Krishna does not happen instantly, there is a journey that unfolds before she turns to Him. First there is the horror of being violently abused by

Dushasana, then there is the desperate plea to her husbands and Kuru elders. After, she frantically runs from one place to the other trying to hold on to her sari. One by one her hopes are broken, and she realises there is nowhere left to turn. It is only Krishna who can deliver her. The firm knowledge that we are helpless cannot be manufactured through mere mental understanding. It has to be a solid inner conviction that defines our life. There are two ways in which this arises: either we face a brutal catastrophe that destroys all that we took for granted, or we become gradually exhausted and frustrated with our desires.

Often the sheer severity of a single incident is enough to wake us up. We can spend a lifetime developing a fixed perspective, we can build beliefs and principles upon which we think everything operates, then suddenly in one event it all comes crashing down. What we thought to be real and true collapses. In such a crisis, we are struck with the truth that everything will be taken away from us and that nothing lasts. Acute situations make life stand still and allow us to see what is behind the curtain. Material existence is recognised for what it is – fickle. One minute it is offering flowers, the next it is throwing stones. Just like Draupadi cannot depend on her husbands or the Kuru elders, we too understand that the world around us cannot be trusted.

Sometimes a one-off major incident does not leave enough of an impression. We still have too many hopes, too many desires and aspirations. No matter how much we are told the material world does not last, we do not feel it. There are still goals that we want fulfilled and plans that have to manifest. Despite knowing how limited they are, we cannot simply drop our baggage and bow before the Divine. Before Draupadi turns to Krishna, she goes on a journey. She runs to the Pandavas, to Bhishma and Drona and sees the shameful expressions on their faces. One after the other, she tries every possible option. When we are loaded with desires we need to be exhausted. Life needs to show us directly how each avenue is a dead end that will never yield lasting happiness. Circumstances have to drain us of our effort and aspiration. Like an overactive child, we have to be worn out.

When different options for happiness are laid out in front of us, we have the chance to approach each one with tremendous energy and enthusiasm. We plan with extreme care, push as much as we can, and then finally we see that despite all that we have done, we have ultimately achieved nothing. Over time the fruitless efforts and broken dreams wear us down and gradually bring us to a place of wisdom. Only after repeatedly going through this do we see the foolishness in trying to force our desires upon life. Eventually, we see that investing in the ways of the world is futile.

How severe and how long this saga goes on for depends on how unconscious we are and how strong the ego is. If we are spiritually aware, the smallest disturbance is enough to wake us up. Quickly, we will be brought to the realisation that ultimately nothing is in our hands. To those who are particularly sensitive, no calamity is needed at all. Just by witnessing the lives of others, they can come

to this helpless state. Every one of us has, or can think of individuals who are facing extremely challenging times. If we are wise we will not simply sympathise with their difficulties, we will recognise the possibility of ourselves in that situation. We will see that the same material reality that inflicts hardship on them is the same material reality we are naively enjoying.

Just because we are comfortable and life is good, we do not become complacent and trust it. The challenges of people, even if they are a world away from our own, can enlighten and make us understand that we are giving all our attention to something that is so treacherous and shallow. By seeing the calamities of others who have placed their hand in the fire, we will understand the truth without having to burn ourselves in the process. But without this awareness, we need to feel the pinch of life directly.

In the previous chapters we have seen that failed aspirations may not always lead to helplessness. They instead create depression and negativity. The hurt can make us recoil into ourselves and withdraw from our path. Real helplessness does not mean running away and hiding from life. It is not to be confused with the condition of Dhritarashtra, who claims helplessness as a cover for cowardice and irresponsibility. Real helplessness does not seek to give up on life, it looks to make it all about the Divinity that lies beyond. It is the admission that we have no other refuge.

Letting Go of the World Means Letting Go of the Ego

There are only two realities, the spiritual and the material. When we are able to strongly reject the material world, the spiritual is all that is left. There is no other choice and no back up plan on the table other than the spiritual path. This understanding makes us one pointed and sincere. If we can still see ourselves enjoying material ambitions, then we will struggle to have exclusive dedication. When things get tough, if opportunities to fulfil these desires come our way, the ego will use them for comfort. If the world is still an option, there will always be a temptation to abandon our path if tests become too intense.

As we lose trust in the material world, the ego's hold also loosens. Its ability to control our behaviour withers away. Slowly the presence of the Divine becomes more perceivable. Gratitude is a key symptom of this. Nothing around us is taken for granted. The lustful grabbing for what is pleasurable is replaced by an immense appreciation for life. Everything is seen as a gift, the food we have, our health, our relationships and even the very fact we exist are all treasured. Helplessness compels us to value every part of life.

The ego tries to tell us we have earned and deserve what we have, but now we see better. No matter how much effort we have put in, we cannot claim ownership over our possessions. All our success is because we stand on the shoulders of innumerable individuals and generations before us. Our parents, friends, the society we live in have all worked together to give us opportunities. What right do we have to say we have achieved anything? We see that the success we have enjoyed has nothing to do with us.

For the conscious individual, helplessness is not a technique or a perspective to be taken; it is an indisputable fact. No one can deny that we are hopelessly subject to the ways of this world.

The deepening of these realisations shifts our focus from the transient to the eternal. A maturity arises where we become inspired to find that cause of all causes, the thing that does not change. Our existence is no longer defined by the enjoyment of this world, we must strive for what is beyond. Helplessness compels us to search and depend on divine grace alone.

Draupadi Calls for Krishna – When Helplessness Awakens the Longing for God

No matter how terrible things become, none of the warriors will respond to Draupadi's plea. In the climax of desperation, she finds another way. The certainty that everyone has abandoned her makes Draupadi turn to the one person who will not. She transforms calamity into an opportunity and calls out to Krishna.

When we are truly helpless, what stops us collapsing into depression and a purposeless void is the value we have for ourselves. We do not want to wallow in negativity, we believe we are better than this. No matter how bad things get, we are not willing to give in. We will not abandon the fight for our survival. For us, life is not meant to be lived in darkness and emptiness. On a deeper level we see we have been born for a reason and we know we have to attain something higher. Amongst the turmoil, there is a determination to thrive. From desperation emerges a tremendous courage and a strong fighting spirit that seeks to make things right. We have to find a way, and even if it means a drastic transformation, we must do it. The utter dissatisfaction with the world combined with the determination to fulfil our life, causes us to go deep and long for something beyond.

Real spiritual fulfilment and material pleasure are diametrically opposed. Like oil and water, they cannot mix. Intensity for the Divine will always be diluted by desires for the world. If Bhima or Bhishma had stepped in to rescue Draupadi, her crisis would be over. Her insult would be avenged and there would be no need for Krishna. In the same way, if we manage to get what we want, if our ego becomes satisfied, then we will not have the strength or inclination to long for something higher. The fulfilment of desires imprisons us in the rat race of material existence. It makes us have faith in the game of life and keeps us blind to the supreme reality.

When we understand this, the dead ends and failed ambitions will not be viewed as an injustice but an act of grace. We will see such disappointments as the dropping of excess baggage. We will not curse our misfortune but celebrate our chance to be free. This is the point where Draupadi calls out "Govinda". Whilst the doors around us are closing, we can feel that the heaven above is opening.

Being helpless makes us feel insignificant and unworthy. Ordinarily we would view this as a terrible thing. But this is only true if it is felt in relation to the world. If we feel that we are not good enough in our relationships or career, there is a problem. We can descend into self-hatred and a whole web of negative emotion.

In this scenario however, this state is not only acceptable but essential. As we become smaller, the Divine becomes larger. This shift gives us wisdom which allows us to perceive something astounding. The Divinity we trust in, is not simply a principle, an energy or a presence, it is a personality. It is God.

The feeling of being undeserving is a recognition of the magnitude of His glory. It does not come from the ego looking at our weaknesses, it comes from beholding the immensity of God's presence. His grace is so powerful and merciful that we cannot help but feel utterly humbled by it. Just like a candle in front of the sun, all our greatness disappears in the light of divine majesty.

Knowing this automatically intensifies the longing for the Divine. By realising the world is not our home, we see that God is, and the more we see it, the more we want to reach Him. Helplessness starts with the brutality of life but matures into the joyous praise of God. As time passes, we renounce the pleasures of the world not just out of detachment or obligation, but as a by-product of our devotion. The more we sample a higher taste, the more we naturally let go of lower pleasures.

Eventually our happiness lies solely with the Divine. The desires we once had, start to become insignificant. The stark contrast between the eternal and the material becomes clear. God's magnificence stirs our heart and becomes the primary motivation for all that we do. In the beginning, our actions were geared to fulfilling particular dreams. Now they are done to honour our relationship with our Beloved. We do not retire into a cave and shun humanity. Life instead, becomes one big arena where we can serve Him.

The goal of our path is not about perfecting ourselves for the sake of being perfect. We are not trying to control the senses and mind to be great yogis. Nor do we act selflessly to be a moral person. We are good because without being good, we will not be able to see God. Our actions become a natural reflection of our relationship. Because we want to feel Him more, we make sacrifices and we become more disciplined. We understand that to know the nature of the Supreme Truth, we have to be qualified and we have to earn it.

This growing attraction to God leads to immense trust, not just that He exists, but that He exists for us. There is a profound confidence in our relationship with Him. He is really there, He is listening, watching and waiting. We are not just a devotee who witnesses Him, but one who walks with Him. We do not simply have faith that He can save, we have faith that He can save us. His grace is available and it is there for the taking. This kind of trust is not blind. We are not holding our breath and hoping for the best. We have been drawn close enough to God to actually perceive the end result. We can smell what is cooking behind the scenes. There is no guesswork or speculation, we know the Ultimate is waiting for us.

Draupadi Lets Go of Her Sari – When Helplessness Leads Us to Surrender of the False Identity

Draupadi understands now that it is only Krishna she can depend on. She repeatedly shouts His name hoping He will respond. All the while Dushasana is still tormenting her. He grabs her sari, and she does her best to cling onto it. She fights for her honour while still calling out to her Lord. Eventually a tremendous peace overcomes her. She lets go and places both hands in the air. The struggle is over. Dushasana laughs as the rest of the Kauravas jeer him on. Draupadi continues to call for Krishna, yet this time she is not shouting but whispering within herself. Her eyes are closed, and the chaos of the gambling hall vanishes. Dushasana continues to pull her sari, but as he does, endless cloth appears. The whole assembly is struck with wonder. Draupadi's humiliation is over and only she understands who has saved her.

Helplessness brings sincere longing and now that longing has brought us into the presence of God. Nonetheless, there is a difference to trusting God and having Him decisively intervene in our life. We have been given the mercy to know Him, but this is not the end of the story. We are waiting for the saving grace to take us to Him. This grace reorganises the circumstances of our life and paves the way forward. It is where God wipes the slate clean and takes full control.

Throughout Draupadi's pleas, Krishna has been listening but not acting. He has been available but has not interceded. Her frantic running from Dushasana and the tight gripping of her sari has prevented Him from revealing Himself. While calling out to Krishna, she is still instinctively trying to preserve her honour.

It is this deep-rooted instinct that needs to be thrown aside. For God to take charge, there must be the complete abandonment of all our ideas and attachments. We can realise the shallowness of the material world, we can see that everything will perish. We can understand that ultimately we have nothing, and there is no other refuge, yet the ego remains. The disturbing presence of Duryodhana is still there and there is still a chance he can capture us. There comes a point when longing has to transform into complete surrender. When we are on the brink of reaching God, the need to move beyond the ego intensifies. The more we progress towards Him, the more urgent it becomes to leave everything behind. Draupadi's climatic struggle with Dushasana illustrates what it is to be on the threshold of heaven. Her persecution shows what happens when the remnants of desire and doubt have still not left us.

Despite God being our greatest joy, we still have our own will. Although we have no big plans to fulfil in the world, we have preferences, tastes, likes and dislikes. We have an attachment to being independent. This is the false identity, the subtle desire to be the doer and enjoyer of material experience. Dushasana is the last attempt of the ego to keep us enslaved. We think we can escape it, but it chases us wherever we go. Eventually Draupadi is forced to face him head on. She appeals to Krishna again and again, but calling is not enough. We have to give ourselves to Him.

Draupadi desperately holds on to her sari. She believes it is all she has to protect her modesty. We too have the same attachment to our false identity. Letting go of it feels like we will be lost into oblivion. At the same time, we have reached a critical point on the spiritual path where this identity has become the final barrier to grace. When the world is our home, the false identity becomes our fundamental asset; when God is our destination, it becomes the burden preventing entry to His abode. To drop our identity is extremely difficult. The more we fight it, the stronger it becomes, no matter how determined we are, it cannot be bullied into submission.

Dropping the false identity does not mean we have to destroy it. The longing for God that has brought us to this point, has made us realise something fundamental – we are not who we think we are. Yearning for the Divine is not mental, or even emotional, it comes from a place much deeper within, it comes from the soul. The stronger it is, the less we identify with the false version of ourselves and the more we align with who we truly are.

The aim is not to perfectly control our mind or remove the sense of being the doer of actions, but to see ourselves as outside them. However convincing the false identity is, it is not us. When all impressions have been exhausted out of us, when the glory of God dwarfs the pleasure of the world, the deluded understanding that we are our likes and dislikes or the bundle of thoughts in our head, starts to fade. The prospect of handing over the false identity in full surrender is no longer a terrifying step. The intense fear of disappearing into a black hole, is replaced by a deep desire to unite with the Person who embodies everything we want.

Crucially, Draupadi does not care what happens to her. Now she is not calling to Krishna to be saved from the Kauravas, she is calling to Krishna to be with Krishna. In the process of surrendering we are not bothered by the outcome, there is no agenda. Who we believed we were is of no importance because who we are to God is all that matters. As a result, we willingly place ourselves entirely in His hands. Just as Draupadi realises she does not need to fight anymore, we see there is nothing to hold onto. Whether we suffer or are successful, it is irrelevant. The world is obsolete, and the only thing that matters is us and God. When we let go of the false identity, naturally the ego which is built upon it disintegrates. Dushasana cannot harm us and Duryodhana has no power to wield. The various impressions, the insecurities and fantasies all wither away. At last there are no more games or dramas to contend with. Finally we are free, we are sincere and we are pure.

Just as Draupadi's shouts turn into a whisper, when we reach the place of surrender, the longing stops being a cry for mercy and changes into a blissful enjoyment. Our yearning for God transforms into the attainment of God. Surrender happens not out of fear or desire but because God is God and we are who we are; the two constitutionally belong together. There is no reason for this relationship, it just is. In the same way that Krishna supplies endless amounts of sari, when we let go of the false identity, God clothes us with His grace. We are no longer an independent person in the material world, but a perfect instrument of His will. We act not because we have something to gain, but because there is nothing else to do other than serve Him.

As Draupadi closes her eyes, the gambling hall, the Kauravas and even the Pandavas no longer exist. The good and the bad disappear, it is the end, and only Krishna remains. Surrender is the giving back of what always belonged to God. We are spiritual beings who have been helplessly trapped in a material realm. The world has stolen us away, and now the Lord's property has been returned.

Reaching the Helpless State of Draupadi

• Meditate on Death and Make It Your Friend

Most of us go through life acting like we are immortal. Hardly anyone lives as if death could come at any moment. While there is a need to be practical and to plan ahead for the future, alongside this there must be the understanding that we will die. This takes no leap of faith or profound reasoning, it is perhaps the one thing we know for sure. Such an important truth cannot be brushed under the carpet, it must be held and even treasured.

Death must become our friend. Focusing on our end is not supposed to bring depression or anxiety but rather an extraordinary clarity in how we see life. Time becomes a precious commodity that cannot be wasted. Our minds become finely tuned towards what is important. That which does not last cannot be invested in.

Meditating on death is actually meditating on God, because it automatically makes the material world secondary. It causes us to bow to the Truth of life and reprioritise everything in the right way. When the knowledge that our days are numbered hits us hard, immediately we are provoked into asking serious questions. 'Why do I exist?' 'Is this all there is?' 'Who am I really?' all become intense points of inquiry. They are like swords that cut through the facade of normal living and penetrate right to the root of the human condition.

Practical Step: Think about death everyday. Contemplate on how everything you have and all the people around you will eventually leave you. Be aware this can happen at any time. Use this, to appreciate the life you have.

- **Learn to Value Yourself in the Right Way**

To value yourself, is to understand what you are worth and to act on it. It means having tremendous determination to make sure we attain what is rightfully ours. At first sight, it sounds like a statement of pride, and certainly it can be. Like Duryodhana, the ego can use this sentiment for name, fame and glory. But in a deeper sense it is the ability to always thrive no matter what life throws at us.

Valuing ourselves means there is no question of giving up when things are hard, there is no temptation to just survive and put up with a meaningless life. We are willing to take risks, we are willing to gamble because we know we were born to experience something beyond. What that is exactly may not be clear, but deep down there is the conviction that we are eternal and we belong somewhere higher.

When Dhritarashtra laments in helplessness he makes almost no sincere effort to change. He sits back and plays the victim. Draupadi however, never stops trying; she is willing to do whatever it takes. The claim of helplessness only becomes legitimate at the end of all effort, not before. We cannot turn to God after a half-hearted attempt. Once we have given everything and placed all that we are before Him, then we have the right to ask for shelter.

When we value ourselves in the right way, we honour the Divine within us and we will go as far as needed. We do not exist to have second rate, cheap goods. Only the ultimate, most exalted Personality can satisfy our soul. We are clear that we cannot settle for what is normal, because fundamentally we are not normal, we are a divine being. We may not have any direct realisation, but we have the sure faith that we are spiritual in nature, and only the source of that nature can bring us freedom.

<u>Practical Step</u>: Remember what you are – a transcendent part of God. Enjoy what is in this world, but do not be satisfied with what it can give you. Reserve that satisfaction for God alone.

• **Protect the Longing of Your Heart at All Costs**

The combination of meditating on death and valuing ourselves automatically leads to desiring God. This desire needs to be protected and nurtured. Few people in the world seriously seek to realise the purpose of their life. To be on the spiritual path wanting to know God is a sure sign of divine grace. We cannot take this for granted. Longing for God is our most important asset, it allows us to endure difficult times and strive for something higher.

If we are not careful, the ego can easily overshadow this longing. Habits are crucial to maintain the level of intensity. Spiritual practice as well as a disciplined routine all help to physically gain control of the situation. The spiritual path is about building momentum, and performing our practice is like offering wood into the fire – it keeps the desire for God alive.

What we learn from Draupadi is that sincere longing for God does not come from our mind, it is a call from our soul. In other words, it is a transcendent quality. We need to pay attention to it, to meditate on what it means and where it is coming from.

As we do this, we will discover a place within, which is not our personality or our ego or even our false identity. It is the Self, who we truly are. This discovery loosens the attachment to the other aspects of our being. We no longer become convinced that we are an independent person in this world, but the soul who is dependent on God.

Practical Step: At all times remember that whether you perceive it or not, your soul is longing to know God, this is why you have come to this path.

Contemplate on the series of events that have brought you to this point. See how everything has been perfectly orchestrated. At some level you have invoked all these situations into your life. Because deep down inside you want something beyond. Understand that part of yourself. When you analyse the mystery behind this longing, you will discover who you are.

Krishna Speaks to Draupadi

You were a queen of the greatest kingdom, now you have become a beaten slave of this material world. How quickly things can turn, how fragile success is. You run to the feet of kings and teachers. Each time you are brimming with hope, and each time you are betrayed. So many promises and lies coming from every part of the room. They fan your expectations and then destroy them. Now you see you cannot trust these people, you cannot trust this world!

You keep fighting, but you do not realise that your determination for yourself is your unripe devotion for Me. You know you were not born to die but to live with Me. As the world closes in, you sense a presence. The clouds disperse and the heavens bellow out 'Govinda!' Now that you have seen My face, you have the highest reason to live. This dark depressing world is made transcendent by your service to Me. Come under My mountain and see there are no curses, only gifts and blessings delivered by My hand.

But you are still being chased. You have taken shelter, but your head has yet to reach My feet. You know Me but you are not with Me. Fear is gripping your mind as you stand on the cliff edge. You see Me well enough, would I ever leave you to fall into the chasm? Your vision of happiness cannot compare with what I am ready to give you. Creation has been waiting for this moment. Look closely and see that you want what I want. Why else would you long for Me? Trust Me and jump.

*****

Now joy and sorrow are one and the same. Without fear you let go of the sari and see the truth that has always been, that you are owned, supported and controlled by Me. I clothe you in My effulgence and supply all that you need. Finally, you reach the abode, the sanctum sanctorum, the holy of holies, the inner chamber of My Heart.

Defeating the Ego with Helplessness

Getting out of hypocrisy is what the whole spiritual path is about. It is a journey from personality to the soul, from unconsciousness to full consciousness, from the world to God. But we need not wait until we have reached a pure surrendered state to rise above hypocrisy. Reaching for helplessness is something we should be looking to do at all times. The many faces of the ego are like barriers that need to be climbed over. Each one has its unique challenge, and so requires a particular aspect of helplessness to cross over it. To put it more precisely, the state of Draupadi has to triumph over the state of all the other characters described. Once we have identified the patterns of the ego, we need to know how to be helpless in each one.

When we understand how transient life is, the pleasure that drives the ego of Duryodhana needs to be seen as meaningless. The gratitude for the path we have been given should make us take responsibility and avoid the ego of Dhritarashtra. The humility and acceptance that arises must prevent the bitter resentment of Gandhari. As we become helpless, our innocence should not allow us to be seduced by the cunningness of Shakuni. The security of an inward connection with the Divine can make us avoid falling into Bhishma's dogmatism. Finally the sincere longing for God makes us clear about our path and we do not have to be led astray by Karna's sympathetic emotions.

These personalities alert us to the complexities of the ego and the vigilance we need to foster. Although they may influence and even control our behaviour, the more we know them, the more we will see that they are not actually us. Knowledge of the characters allows us to isolate our negative qualities and recognise who we are outside of them. Instead of being consumed by them, we can keep them at a distance. This is the fruit of self-analysis.

When we first see how the ego has been working within us, it is easy to judge ourselves and feel dejected. But as we have already seen with Draupadi, if we can view these insights in the right way, the lack of hope places our head at the feet of God. The aim of the spiritual path is not about trying to eliminate the ego, it is about understanding that only God can. Rigidly attempting to reach some perfect pure state by ourselves is delusory. If anything, it closes the door to the Divine and runs the risk of empowering the ego even more.

We must remember that sincerity is not some far away goal. It is our natural state. Despite all our flaws, somewhere inside us we do want God. Our dharma is to rediscover that desire and make it grow to the point where we are ready to throw our hands up in the air.

God is watching and waiting to seize that moment. Only when we have analysed enough, worked enough and longed enough, will His grace make the change. Then we will know what life really is, we will know what Love really is and we will know who God really is.

The Master

When you meet a personality who is able to physically respond to your deepest thoughts and desires, you know you have encountered an individual who can respond to prayers. When you meet someone who is able to inform and prepare you for future events, you know you have met someone who is a master of time and space. When you follow someone who is able to identify and destroy your fantasy and ego, you know you are with someone who cares not for your praise but only your advancement. When you see someone who tirelessly works to uplift you, you are with someone who embodies unconditional Love. When someone's mere presence removes worldly attraction and awakens a longing for God, you know you have met a true Master.

We cannot understand divine Love with our minds, but we can know it through the impact it has on our lives. It does not merely inspire and care for us, it challenges our limitations and shakes our negativity. Love by its nature pushes us to grow and fulfil our ultimate potential. It does not play the game of the ego nor does it bow to our material desires.

When the time is right, this Love enters our life as the Master. It comes because at the deepest level we have asked for it.

A true Master looks at us, not as people around us do, not even as we do, but as God does. He is never on the side of who we are, but on who we could be. The Master works tirelessly for our growth, He has no interest in name and fame. He sees the obstacles in the way and He understands the shortest route through it. Exposing the ego is not the work of somebody who is out for justice, but of one who is longing to liberate. Whether we glorify or crucify Him, makes no difference. The Master has nothing to gain yet He never stops serving. He is full and cannot be added to in any way, yet He willingly sacrifices for our welfare. Who can understand what truly motivates Him? How can we know the mystery of Love?.

The insights in this book are not based on speculation or theoretical ideas, but on innumerable experiences with Paramahamsa Vishwananda. They have come from witnessing divine Love in action, from being with a personality who is ready to give God to anyone who wants Him.

I hope this book has helped you in some way to march forward on your path.

May the Blessings of the Master be Upon Us All.

Krishna Speaks to Duryodhana

You are lying here alone this night because the world you worked so hard for has left you.

Now do you see the treachery of pleasure? Think about how you tried to rule and conquer, how everything was used and abused for your glory.

You have been chasing shadows and trying to capture air. Your hunger cannot be appeased with fantasies and delusions of greatness.

Even now I can see you are growing numb to the thrills. Your body is exhausted from the endless running. What will you do when you reach the top of the mountain? You will only search for a bigger one to continue the madness.

So catch your breath for a few moments and ask 'Who Are You?'

Look again. Yes,

you see it. Behold its wonder and effulgence blazing in all directions. This is not pleasure, this is Me. Now that you know it, what will you do? Can the world ever look the same? I have shown you gold, so throw away the stones. Choose Me instead of the army.

You know the aimless road of a conqueror but not the flight of a servant. It is time to mature – why look for joy, when the source of joy is waiting for you? Yes, you will need to be committed. Yes, you will need sacrifices. But did you expect the ultimate prize to be given away so cheaply?

Give up trying to bind Me, and instead walk with Me. You cannot doubt the possibility, for your very existence is proof that this is your destiny.

****

Krishna Speaks to Dhritarashtra

Sitting on your throne you only pretend to be blind, for you have seen more than what is needed. Dharma is staring you in the eyes waiting for you to respond.

Surely even you are not convinced by your own lamentation. Any excuse, any story to keep you in your cave. You love the quiet. Everything is where you want it, there you can remain in your slumber, undisturbed by the turbulence of the world.

Tick Tock. Tick Tock.

There goes life and still you are not afraid. Why do you delay? Can you not see that living in denial is not living? The veil of deceit is wearing thin, so step out of the shadows and take your place. I have laid a banquet and your seat is reserved. But I will not dress you or brush your hair. I will not prepare your clothes or shine your shoes. The invitation has been sent and your carriage awaits, but you must claim it before it passes.

Once you taste the food I have prepared, your eyes will return. You will know the sweetness of what it is to serve. No more a beggar, but a prince at the table of his father. See the delights that are on offer and think of the dark cave you left behind. Now your potential is unleashed, I have made you anew. You are an ambassador of My Love and people are tasting my glory through you. Now use your new vision and see that you have your dharma, you have yourself and now you have Me.

****

Krishna Speaks to Gandhari

You have been carried on a bed of roses and now you have been dropped. The shock of a shattered dream is a heavy burden. But can you not see the other door which has opened? Look at the light pouring out, this is your chance to meet me. The world has abandoned you so that I can rescue you. Your bag has been stolen so you are free to hold my hand.

But for that you have to get up off your knees. Because you have covered your eyes all you have is the memory of rejection. Do not confuse dragging yourself along the ground with progress. This is not heroism, but deceit. Frustration is building and you realise your austerity has been for nothing. Calm your rage, throw aside your self-pity and see that this all has meaning.

Life is not cruel, this is not a conspiracy but an opportunity, it is just your soul reaching for something higher. Do not deny its right. Accept. Make peace and turn once again to that door. Take off your veil, not to look at your son, but to look at Me. Now your eyes are open, can you see that the snakes were actually ropes for you to meet me above.

How could I be against you, when I am the only one who can stand with you? When you see that eternity is on offer, you will understand the price was so small. When you behold the magnitude of Myself on a plate, then you will know that nothing was asked of you.

Krishna Speaks to Shakuni

The humiliation of your sister has turned you into a pauper amongst kings. You want to wear their clothes and eat their food. Without any shame you are willing to sell your soul to do it. You hide behind pillars whispering and listening to echoes. Thinking, watching and plotting, is there nothing you would not sacrifice for your nephew?

As you pick up your dice, you know what you are doing. Throw by throw the blessings I have given you are being cast aside. Do not disgrace yourself for the sake of cheap fame. Without any care for dharma, you take fake pearls and sell them to the gullible. Who can trust your words? Can you even trust yourself?

Amongst all the excitement of the game, you have forgotten I exist. Put aside the dice and place your palms together. Abandon the conspiracy and come to My altar. There is no need to think, no need to explain, the heart has a different language. It is simple and innocent. It is Truth and how different it is! You underestimated Me all along, now you have a glimpse of the larger picture that never ends. You thought you knew it. Now you see that there is nothing to conquer with the mind and everything to gain with your soul.

Krishna Speaks to Bhishma

Standing like a white lion in your silver-plated armour the whole world is bowing to your virtue. No doubt you are near to Me but are you dear? No one can fault you, no one can surpass your example. But the law is your God, not Me. The thunderous sound of your conch on the battlefield drowns out My voice in your heart. You are fighting, but against whom? Arrows defend an army, as rules protect the path, but your weapons are being fired at Me not for Me.

I do not love you because you can command an army or because you can slay any enemy, but because you belong to me and nothing you do can change that. Realise this and lower your bow for a moment. Give up your attachment to what you ought to be and be who you truly are. I am not the tyrant in the sky, I am your friend, your very breath. Let us smile, dance and laugh together like we once did.

I am not asking you to step off your chariot, I only want you to ride it on my side. Love Me then fight for Me, but do not fight to love Me. You already wear all the jewels of a devotee and after I place My soul in your heart, I will hold you up so all can see you are Mine

Krishna Speaks to Karna

You do not know who you are and it is haunting you wherever you look. This perennial question has come to define your life. You should have raised it up to the heavens for Me to answer, but you took the fake alternative. The great son of the Sun is now begging for affection from anyone who will give it. Like a man with no home, you scurry around meekly bowing before every request.

You do not belong to the people, you belong to Me. Foolishly you believe you have it all worked out, but your path was ordained by Me long ago. I wrote every detail of it. Falling for a heroic fantasy you have chosen your own road, and with your shining armour and earrings you want to save the world. Your shallow romance with humanity has stopped you reaching for My grace. Let Me take hold of your chariot wheel to stop this crusade.

Yes there is suffering in the world, but who has the solution, you or I? I am Love. What can you hope to give others if you do not have Me? I will teach you not to help but to transform. You think that what I am giving you is for yourself, but no, my dear, it is for humanity. I will fill you with Love and once the vessel is full, I will keep going. From that flow, all of life will taste this nectar. Now see the Truth, that when you serve Me, you serve all that is, in the highest way. Stop asking who you are. The answer is obvious – you are part of Me.

 MAYURAN SENTHILNATHAN is a speaker for the Bhakti Marga organization and the author of 'Avatars of the Master'. He is the creator of the Dharma Speaks YouTube channel which focuses on explaining Indian philosophy and spiritual practice. His particular passion lies in unveiling the wisdom of ancient Vedic stories. Using profound insights, he is able to draw out their beauty and provide key lessons for seekers of all backgrounds.